As They Were

As They Were

A. PETER DEWEY

Introduction by Nancy Dewey Hoppin

Epilogue by Geoffrey T. Hellman

BAUHAN PUBLISHING
PETERBOROUGH, NEW HAMPSHIRE
2024

ISBN: 978-087233-386-4
Library of Congress Control Number: 2024934729

Note: While the original text in its entirety is A. Peter Dewey's, the photographs (some of which were taken by Peter at the time) and the captions have been added for this edition.

Cover and book design by Henry James

BAUHAN PUBLISHING
PETERBOROUGH NEW HAMPSHIRE
WWW.BAUHANPUBLISHING.COM

Printed in the United Kingdom

EPIGRAPH

OFTEN AFTER curfew he [Adrian Goekoop] would take the entire orchestra from the night club Schéhérazade home with him as well as the dancers and singers, cold chickens, magnums of champagne and any officer and his companions who wished to come whether he was known or not. I remember riding through Paris lying (with a British aviator) on the rack affixed to the roof of a taxi, the inside being full; as we watched the branches pass between us and the gray moonlit sky overhead, he discussed his fear and consciousness of death in the strange impersonality he must have felt in such unusual surroundings.

—A. PETER DEWEY, 1939 from page 69

CONTENTS

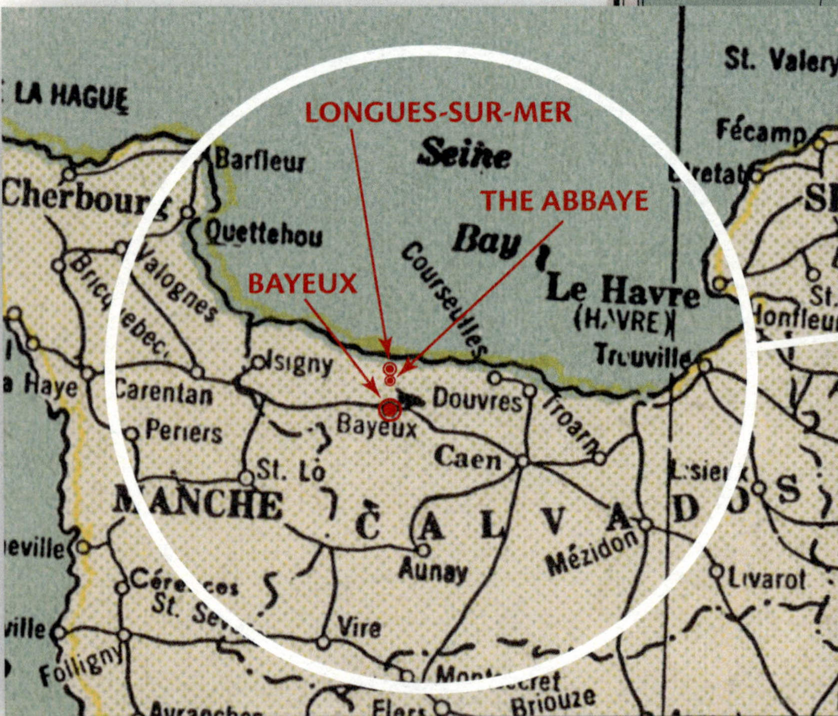

1939 Map of France *(right)* with detail showing the location of the Abbaye *(above)*

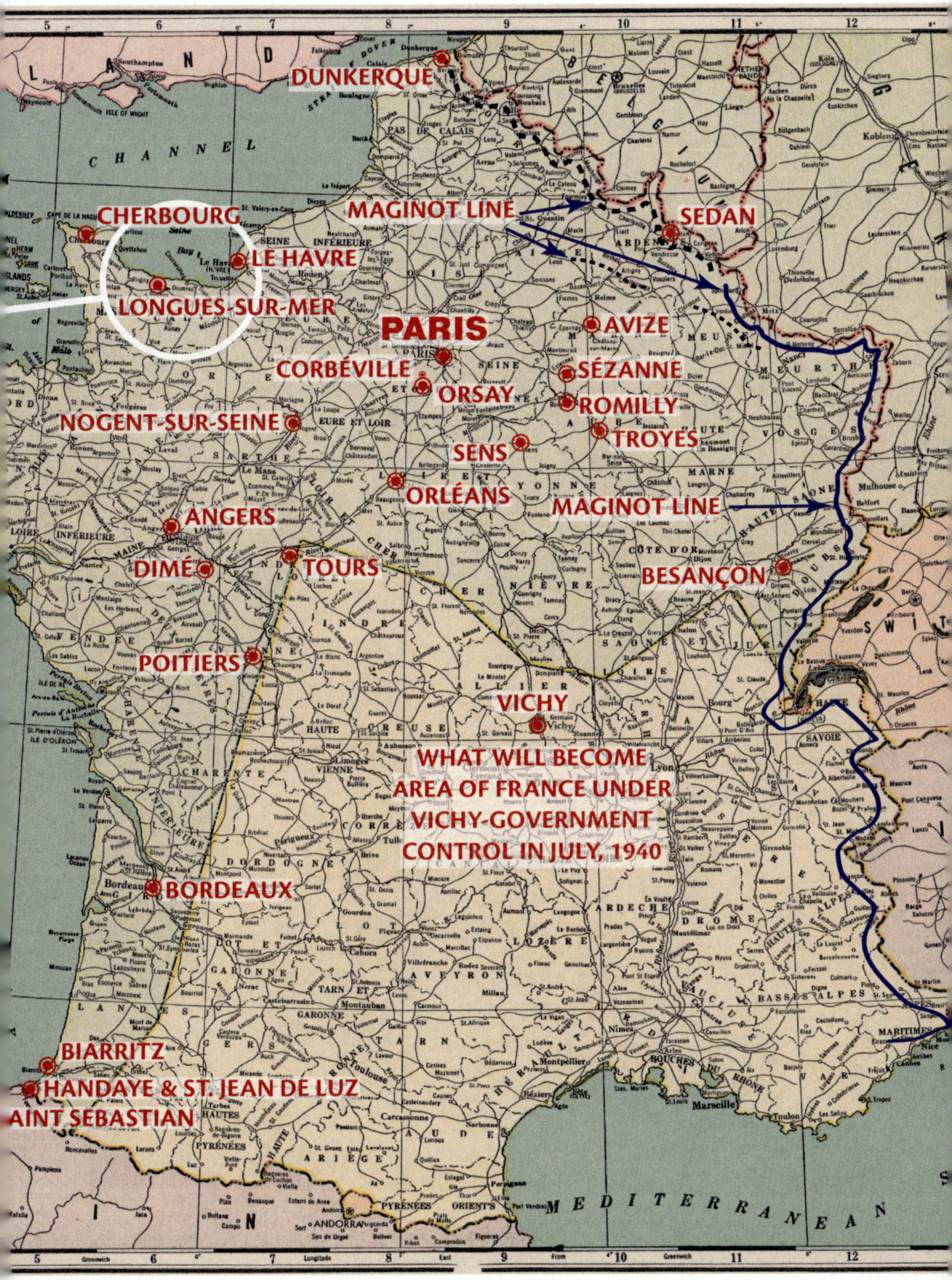
DUNKERQUE
MAGINOT LINE
SEDAN
CHERBOURG
LE HAVRE
LONGUES-SUR-MER
PARIS
AVIZE
CORBÉVILLE
SÉZANNE
ORSAY
ROMILLY
NOGENT-SUR-SEINE
TROYES
SENS
ORLÉANS
MAGINOT LINE
ANGERS
DIMÉ
TOURS
BESANÇON
POITIERS
VICHY
WHAT WILL BECOME
AREA OF FRANCE UNDER
VICHY-GOVERNMENT
CONTROL IN JULY, 1940
BORDEAUX
BIARRITZ
HANDAYE & ST. JEAN DE LUZ
AINT SEBASTIAN
CHANNEL
MEDITERRANEAN

Peter's parents walking at the Abbaye after the war

INTRODUCTION

My FATHER, Peter Dewey, participated in some of the most dramatic and important episodes of World War II. *As They Were* opens a window onto daily life in France during the "*drôle de guerre,*" "phony war," "*sitzkrieg,*"—those months of nervous waiting for war to begin that many have forgotten or have never known about.

Peter was in Paris on September 3, 1939, when France and England declared war on Nazi Germany. As US nationals were advised to leave France if they had "no urgent reason to stay," Peter accompanied his parents, Charles and Suzette Dewey, home to Chicago. However, he "was determined to return to my stricken love, my second land," France. He had graduated from Yale that May, been an editor of the *Yale Daily News* and was writing a novel set in France. A tip from his brother Bud (Charles S. Dewey Jr.) helped him find a job as a cub reporter in the Paris office of the *Chicago Daily News*. Before the end of October, Peter, aboard a Pan-Am Clipper, a flying boat, was crossing the ocean again. Upon landing in Lisbon he wrote, "Across a long gangplank I walked (back) into Europe."

Peter was a natural choice for the Paris desk. He was fluent in French; in fact, he stuttered in English, but not in French. He was at ease with the customs and formalities of *ancien régime* Europe as he had lived in Europe much of his early life.

From 1927 to 1931, his father served as financial advisor to the Polish government. Peter was eleven when, just before Christmas, on a cold, clear evening, he and his family arrived by train in Warsaw. Fine lodgings were ready for them; the Polish government had rented the Sobanski Palace for the family's use for the duration of Charles's appointment. At the Palace, the staff was lined up to greet them. When the majordomo bent to his knees to kiss Peter's father's hand, his father, knowing that the man spoke English, said that this was now an American household and would be run with American customs: no more hand kissing.

Peter soon became a Polish Boy Scout. For the next several years he was educated at Institut Le Rosey in Switzerland, returning to Poland for vacations. In 1931 Charles Dewey's appointment to Poland ended. The family returned to their Chicago base. Peter, age fifteen, enrolled at Saint Paul's School in Concord, New Hampshire.

However, although Charles Dewey was no longer serving in any official capacity, his advice was still sought in Europe. (In 1941, he was elected to the US House of Representatives from Illinois's 9th District and served until 1945. From 1948 to 1951 he was agent-general of the Joint Congressional Committee on Foreign Economic Cooperation, the congressional watchdog over the Marshall Plan.) In addition, Suzette had strong family ties to France, especially to Normandy. There were reasons aplenty for the family to embark on what became a life-changing adventure.

So, in 1931, upon leaving Poland, the Deweys bought an abandoned twelfth century Benedictine Abbaye, the Abbaye de Sainte-Marie in the little village of Longues-sur-Mer in Normandy. Bayeux, of Bayeux Tapestry fame, is less than six miles from the Abbaye. Arromanches, where the remains of Mulberry Harbor, one of England's two D-Day floating harbors, can still be seen, is close as well. With guidance from the Ecole des Beaux-Arts, the Deweys restored the Abbaye to loveliness and unprecedented comfort. The Abbaye, which, in Peter's words, "sighed a green ether of mists in a hollow among orchards spiced with white blossoms," became his home of the heart.

After Peter's assassination in 1945 in Saigon, this book was assembled from the writings he left behind, and published by his friends and family. His distinct voice comes through on each page: high-spirited, unafraid, observant, sensitive to those he encounters, it's the voice of a young man who was growing up fast. He writes with feeling about what he sees, sometimes with humor, sometimes with scorn and outrage. Here is the rationing of food, and here too the great meals (with plenty of butter) still available in the great restaurants. Here are damp, penetrating cold, bats dying in the walls, hot water and gasoline shortages, his friends' fears, the feverish gaiety in Paris, the refugees, the sadness but high resolve among the Polish troops. War is coming ever closer. And then, it bursts upon them.

Peter's temperament compelled him to engage, to act. He, with his father's help, was instrumental in creating the American Volunteer Ambulance Service for those Polish fighters who had regrouped, some near Angers, under General Wladyslaw Sikorski. Still, those ambulances had not arrived and there was no news of when they might. Peter, unwilling to wait, joined the Polish Army as an aspirant lieutenant and member of PAVAS (Polish American Volunteer Ambulance Service), organized by his friend Ted Schulze. [Ted was the stepson of Anthony J. Drexel Biddle, the US ambassador to Poland from 1937 to 1943.] On June 9 at night, PAVAS left Paris, and Peter with them, to liaison with the First Tank Brigade of the Polish Army under the command of General Stanislaw Maczek. The Front was moving so rapidly that their ambulances were nearly overrun. The Nazis entered Paris on June 14, five days later. Peter writes of their retreat while being strafed by German and Italian planes:

> Blood and bodies littered the roads and feebly kicking horses bleeding from immense wounds . . . the

> air was thick with the stench of burning flesh and shrieks. The groans in our ambulance gave way to the musty smell of death.
>
> Often we heard . . . of men retreating and empty trucks dashing past them not stopping to pick them up.
>
> It is the sergeants who command us up there, there is no one else, the officers are all gone.

He and his crew offered what aid and transport they could.

Peter managed to cross into Spain on June 25, twelve hours before the Nazis closed that border. Delayed by red tape and interned in Portugal, he finally was permitted to board the *Manhattan*. He sailed for home on July 12.

There is a sadness that comes in reading this book, knowing that five years later Peter's own story would end. *As They Were*, (printed here in its entirety) fascinating for those who want a sense of daily life during the "*drôle de guerre*," introduces the young man that Peter was on his way to becoming. His family ties were strong; letters between Peter and his father, Charles, are warm, relaxed, and filled with sharp, practical analyses of people and situations, political and otherwise. This way of thinking was Charles's own. He encouraged its growth in Peter.

Peter's wartime assignments required him to write frequent intelligence reports. One of his last, to a fellow member of the Office of Strategic Services, contained what was almost a throw-away line: "Cochin-China is burning, the French and British are finished here, and we ought to clear out of Southeast Asia."

But we did not.

And he did not.

—NANCY DEWEY HOPPIN

MAY, 2024

OVERTURE

THESE WRITINGS are indeed Trivia. The entire book is one of ramblings dissociated; facts are interpolated where I think of them and sometimes where they happened for such was the chaos of my months in France. In the lurid, changing light of that mighty transition, I, my friends and acquaintances, and the innumerable people I saw intimately—since they were in pain or occupied with problems of life and death—these faces and voices I saw and heard as marionettes might see one another in the curtained light of their stage; our faces of an unnatural hue, our limbs jerked by the chords of vital emotions in peace almost forgotten. And we chattered together as the glasses and cups and saucers of Lady Mendl's Fridays, or was it Wednesdays, at the Ritz when she received in her magnificent Empire Suite overlooking the Place Vendôme, reminiscently withdrawn from the sand-bagged shrouded column.

There existed a consonance between the vapidity of the Ritz and that of the streets, an Attitude which was to grow more brittle as the leaves grow more brittle in the Fall, more easily blown away as by the storm gathering in the East. Was it the intimations from the East that made people, the faces and voices those of pantomime as memory is pantomime? Such intimations, palpable *fluide* as the French acknowledge the existence of such psychical force with a word, I have felt; the *fluide*, the ecstasy of fear, the odor, the smell of the sweat of fear as forty million people, forty million brittle leaves, blew before the black storm; and the drier ones, the lifeless ones, the useless ones, first in their Rolls Royces and the boutonniéres of the Grand Cordon in their buttonholes. The officers first and the men later; the leaders first, then the people leaving their swine and cows and sheep behind, or their horses struggling in their blood on the tree-lined avenues. Death is often preceded by miasmas and fevers, and in occasional lucidity one may have preternatural discernment before returning to chaos and the milling of the senses. With utmost clarity a voice is remembered and then the rush alone of passing time. Such I was: my days of lucidity and turmoil and with my senses I suffered the sickness, the miasmas with which France was infected, and yet my mind did not interpret their portentousness, and like a child, I felt the wind and the first great drops but did not understand them to be the coming of the storm and the shutters were closed too late to exclude the deafening reverberations of the thunder, the heat and whiteness of the lightning.

I was in France when the War was declared. With my father I had taken the *Ile de France* to land at Le Hâvre the 15th of August. There I had expected the delivery of a car ordered six months before and was vastly disappointed when it failed to appear, as I imagined it might, with a mechanic at the wheel in a dust coat. Instead came Monsieur Leloup, the mechanic of the Citroën Garage at Bayeux at the wheel of our Citroën Commerciale—the French counterpart of a station wagon, since a good sized heifer might be coaxed within should one so wish; or seven seats installed for all members of a peasant's family (from grandpapa, who eats with his straw hat on his head in summer, to bébé, who walks about without trousers underneath his apron).

Such was our Commerciale and such Leloup. The one black with red wheels, the other toothless and grinning and infinitely

A *Commerciale* similar to the Deweys

likable, like a shovel or a duck or a tree; an object dependable, in being the expression of its use. Yes, Leloup was an old Frenchman and might be used and did not have the transcendental atmosphere of intellectuals.

My father got all the luggage into the rear, and I looked hopefully and gave ear for the triple carbureted whine of my car which did not appear and we looked at the city.

Le Hâvre never fails to amaze. It lies so seemingly small and lower than one, as one approaches on a steamer, and the twin stacked *Minotaur*, a tug of ancient vintage, creams the oil-green waters of the outer harbor in much the same manner each year. I remember seeing the snowy triangles of the Royal Yacht Squadron, their white ensigns at the peak sailing out of the English mists into French waters as we docked, but that was many years ago, a day in June when the *Atlantique* was not lying by the pier where her veneered entrails were gutted two years before.

And the amazing Hôtel Frascatti.

But over the cobbles of Le Hâvre we rolled in the Commerciale along the Seine by the chalk cliffs to Quille-Boeuf to take the *bac*, the smoke-snorting ferry, to cross the Seine and enter deep into the foliaged heart of Normandy, deep into a shadowed greenness, fertile in late summer, among fruit and coiled furrows moving under the sun.

Longues, our destination, the sequestrated village where we passed our summers, might harbor unnatural loves, crimes bloody

L'Abbaye de Sainte-Marie à Longues-sur-Mer

and treacherous as the slaying of Siegfried, tragedies dark as the Broody Dane; our Abbaye sighed a green ether of mists in a hollow among orchards, spiced in white blossoms.

When I hear the echoing twitter of a bird flying to a tree to take shelter from an impending rain, I am reminded of the salon of our neighbor, Madame Guichard. On hearing the soft patter of the rain on the terrace she would tell her daughter to rise and shut the windows, not raising her head from her endless sewing. Soon the maître d'hotel would open the salon doors and announce dinner, there would be a stir and we would pass through a twilit entry way, our heels clicking on the marble to gather about the table with its low-hanging French lustre at the middle, and the rain would patter through the warm Summer twilight on the shining laurel leaves and on the grass and gravel of the park.

August 13, 1939, Madame and Monsieur Guichard, my father and the Guichard children, (Chichi who had married Anitchkoff, and Doudouce who was Madame Ste. Marie and barely eighteen, Fido and Hubert) and I, sat about a round table in the Source room of our Abbaye, a vaulted stone room in which was sunk a well perpetually cool and echoing. It was a fine spot for reading, or at six, for cocktails. Yes, a fine spot for cocktails, and Monsieur Guichard told my father there would be a war and my father said, "never."

He had too much faith, perhaps in idealism and the fear of pain and continued sorrow in Europe. He could not believe humanity dead and experience forgotten. A year later Mr. Duell, *Chicago Daily News* correspondent in Berlin, was to tell him Germany felt a sadness as that one might feel did one inadvertently kill one's neighbor and old friend with whom one had rather enjoyed fighting. Perhaps my father was right, perhaps indeed the Germans did not want to kill France, perhaps the *Drang nach Osten* would have satisfied the terrifying vitality inherent in their amoebic stretching growth. Perhaps they did not want another bitter war in French and German grave yards. More recently still, Ambassador Henri-Haye affirmed the obvious; that France was not invaded but made war for a pledged word. But was not the word given to preserve a status quo of benefit to France, and had the word not been given and had the Germans proceeded to the East, might not France have been raped later? But all is lost in surmise, and that which is, or was, is only to be considered and the might have been is not fit subject for example, particularly today.

Perhaps Monsieur Guichard wished to fight, and I noticed that many Frenchmen who had known the last war donned their uniforms like old bucks and swaggered. It was a degeneracy on the part of the old when not patriotic conviction, and how could it be conviction for the victors of 1918? Such a one was Monsieur Guichard who had abandoned holdings in the Argentine in 1914 to return with five children to France and the downing of seven planes. For his efficiency and heroism he received the Belgian Croix de Guerre from Albert himself. The Knight King had once watched Captain Guichard dog fight. After the war Monsieur Guichard suffered the disillusionment of war, not the disillusionment inherent in seeing that it was all for nothing, since any man may know, must know that war is of life, but rather to see men return to peace and the world to peace and one's self to peace, the disequilibrium of unfamiliar peace with its petty treacheries. But in August, 1939, was he glad? Certainly in the shadow of impending war, as a major of aviation reserves the future promised, and he was much happier already, with a grim pleasure, this big Norman gentleman with his gray mustache, and I thought of his two sons and three sons-in-law, some of whom I knew like brothers.

Two days at Longues, then down I went to Paris to get my car at the factory in Suresnes where I had much talk with a Frenchman who told me they were retooling for Pratt and Whitney. But I saw little smoke from the chimneys for the workmen were taking their customary two weeks off in late August as they did all over France, this two weeks before the war. I walked through the idle factory under the airy girders and the atmosphere was much as that of an empty church or concert hall. One feels echoingly alone where one might expect to hear much sound and many people... An idle reminiscence as were my thoughts the afternoon of my return to Longues. I sat at the Grand Corniche at Rolleboise, the Louis XVI restaurant where it was my custom to lunch when traveling Route Nationale 13, or La Route des Quarante Sous, stretching its uneven and, to me, familiar length between Bayeux and Paris. I sat high above the Seine and watched the barges and skiffs leaving a broadening wake like beetles on the water and looked far out on the trim geometry of fields extending to the East beyond. I drank my *rosé* wine and listened to a Frenchman seated with his wife or mistress ask the waiter to bring a plate for his dog. The French treat animals the way we do children, with solicitude but without comprehension. I felt well-fed and happy and fortunate in what I considered to be my great understanding and love for France.

Recently I received a letter from Fido Guichard, the Major's son, in which he sadly wrote, "If we had thought when we saw one another in Longues in August, 1939, that our two properties

(opposite) 1939 Talbot Coupe, the model Peter drove

should be Nazi *Kommandanturs*, as they are now…And yet…?" This from Fido who was a sergeant in the French Army in unoccupied France. But I have accordioned the past and had no intimations of the future at Rolleboise, nor the same night at Longues as Fido may have had as we walked in the rose garden in the company of his sisters.

The following morning, my father and I drove to Cherbourg to meet Mother on the white *Empress of Britain*, now sunk somewhere in the winding sheet of her war paint. The *Empress* didn't come up to the new pier but rode to anchor in the outer harbor while passengers disembarked. From the pilot boat we saw Mother standing at the rail, and we waved happily. We passed a few days in our glowing gardens, in the rose garden by Mother's parasol; the devolution of the few days of peace before I proceeded to Paris with my father who was expected in Warsaw.

In April 1939, Father warned Smygli-Rydz—when we had first known him as one of Pilsudski's colonels he was called Rydz-Smygli. Subsequently he had inverted his name since it signified "little mushroom," a vegetable incompatible with the title of Dictator. Four months before, my father had warned Rydz-Smygli that Poland should be crushed in the event of war and he urged that Poland should not be bellicose. As an alternative to war, he outlined a plan for a corridor which should be made to extend to the right of East Prussia abutting at the port of Memel in exchange for the refusion of East Prussia with Germany. The Marshal had laughed and explained that should the Nazis attack, the Poles without effort would strike to the North. My father shrugged his shoulders

at such optimism, yet submitted his plan to Cardinal Mundelein who in turn relayed it to the Pope: but the Poles, their frontiers guaranteed by Sir Howard William Kennard, His Britannic Majesty's Ambassador to the Zamec, were aggressive and without a doubt did not believe their own secret service, did they possess one, concerning concentrations of Nazi troops in East Prussia. Evidence of an identical sanguinity I had witnessed myself two years before when shooting at Princess Lubomirska's. Her son-in-law, the Prince of Bourbon-Parme, told me unsmilingly that Polish saboteurs were using acid paint on tanks in the German factories, paint which corroded the steel plates of the machines, rendering them vulnerable to guns of the lightest caliber.

Three weeks later I was to witness in Count Potocki's woods to the South in the vicinity of the Czecho-Slovakian border, the tough-looking Polish peasant soldiery on the move prior to the invasion of the coal-bearing Tetsen regions. In so doing they set a precedent for their own subjugation and lost much sympathy. But aggressors believe they can ignore sympathy.

The Poles in Posnania were at the period of which I write not anti-German. Hitler had guaranteed their frontiers. They lived a good life, these *grands seigneurs* whose vast estates were but beginning to be parceled by the powerful peasant party which represented three-quarters of the population, for Poland was seventy-five per cent agricultural. Soon the Poles will be seventy-five per cent even more literally of the earth. Indeed, of Poland, Posnania was the first to suffer for her trust.

My father and I proceeded to Paris. I to drive down to Besançon to visit some friends, feeling very grand in the half-light with a mechanic from Suresnes to adjust my car on the straight roads to the South.

The chateau I had been asked to stop at stood fifteen kilometers behind the Maginot Line, which lies particularly thick and doubled near the Swiss frontier as one might have noted from the maps hanging· in French post offices. I lived an idyllic three days, swimming in the reedy Oignon with friends, from punts chained to ancient willows, for one could not swim against the too rapid current. With cavalry officers I went to Pignerolles and drank Kirsch, and later drove to the Casino at Plombiéres where Napoleon III had his disguised and intricate interview with Cavour. The same night we found ourselves in the salon of an *hôtel particulie*r in Vesoul where lived three sisters with whom we had porto and madeleines threaded on fantasy till it was very late. These nameless encounters, how pleasant they were in unregimented France.

Yet I was virtually without news and decided to return to Paris. My mechanic had deserted me, and I found it difficult to procure sufficient gasoline on the way back. If the dispenser were pleasant, he would give freely, if not, *tant pis*. It was already the end of August and many special classes of reservists were being called. Under crossed Tricolors one read *L'Armée de Terre, L'Armée de Mer, L'Armée del' Air* and such and such a class (with a blank filled with a great number at the bottom denoting the class to be called) must report with stout boots and their helmets of the last war if they had kept them. If they had no stout boots, they must come in slippers since these might be easily stored away while the reservist should be shod at the expense of the Government. Such notices appeared everywhere.

At the barriers of Troyes, I was stopped that I might show my passport and *laissez passer* given me by the Consul General at Chicago, a kindly gentleman since disavowed by the Pétain Government. I was ordered not to enter the town since it was used by the military exclusively. I must take to the country roads in order to reach Paris. In the little out of the way villages, as I skirted the greater towns, women were standing at their doors or near the splashing fountains not doing anything or talking but merely standing and waiting. At every railroad crossing and by the bridges stood guards.

At Paris, the outskirts were crowded with the population of the first evacuation, while at my garage, they were out of gas and gave every evidence of not caring. I left my car and walked to a cafe thinking ruefully of better days.

I have not been more melancholy than at Weber's the third of September. The papers said France would be at war at noon—I believe it was noon—I had a newspaper that I'd purchased and hoped to keep but it was lost. I thought at one time I should have it framed but then the papers seemed so plentiful blowing about the streets… but I do wish I had it now. I sat at Weber's having a cup of tea with an American lady who was very much afraid. The *midinettes* and chasseurs, the news boys, the gentlemen and occasional soldiers, the bicyclists with their bicycle boxes, the cab drivers, the *cocottes*, all the hodgepodge of Parisians of the alert eyes, had their gas mask canisters hanging from their shoulders. Two lovers walked by hand in hand, their gas masks bumping metallically at each step. The sky was of that Parisian lavender Simon understood so well, so consonant with the gray-green of the Bois, the city and the bridge-spanned Seine.

I looked down the rue Royale at the fountains in the Place de la Concorde, splashing amongst the balustrades which I believe have been removed to accommodate German parades; I looked at the fountains, their panache of feathered water, and raised my cup in reaction to emotion. It was twelve o'clock and the world did not end.

Paris was being evacuated and to every city and town trains steamed loaded with refugees.

At Bayeux, Mother, with our neighbors, Daisy de Broglie, the Duchesse d'Harcourt, Madame Foy, Madame Guichard and others, received the refugees, for the most part children who were bedded on straw under the Norman pier arches of the Cathedral of Bayeux till more permanent billets could be found. The cars in all the villages were requisitioned and a sticker with the name of the village from whence they came pasted on the windshield. Children were taken from the Cathedral to the various houses of the villages where space had been previously allocated. Furniture, mugs, plates, napkins, napkin rings, knives and forks and blankets were requisitioned from the shops in exchange for receipts signed by the sub-prefect on the credit of the Government. These articles were in turn signed for by the mayors of the different villages who carried them away in wagons, thus the governmental hierarchy of France functioned admirably in crisis.

The refectory of our Abbaye was transformed into a dining hall for the children and the ancient carpentry of the roof, I am certain, rejoiced to hear gulpings and clatterings reminiscent of the twelfth century. Later during the Winter, the refectory was adjudged as too damp and the children were obliged to leave, for as St. Bernard prescribed, the Abbaye was built in a hollow to derive power from the streams to turn the mill. The Beaux Arts next took it over as a storehouse for the glass of Rouen Cathedral, and after that the German armies of occupation.

The windows of the Abbaye were daubed from the inside with a paint brewed from a blue calcimine and water, and the headlights of the cars were covered with it as well, yet leaving a small square of unveiled glass at the center; Admiral and Mrs. Long, as well as Mr. Max Shoop of Sullivan and Cromwell's and President of the American Club of Paris, agreed to come and live at Longues should they consider it advisable themselves to evacuate Paris.

Mother worked interminably and each refugee was supplied with all the necessaries and comforted, and there were nurses at the stations to relieve mothers of the care of their children and feed them, and everybody worked with a will as at a picnic with the wonderful altruistic realism of the French.

My father was boarding the North Express when the American Embassy at Paris received a wire from Ambassador Biddle at Warsaw saying it was best that he not leave for Poland. After some reflection my father wisely decided to stay in France. The train, stoned in Germany, was the last to pass Stench on the Oder, the German border town, a conjunction of names which amused me very much on my first trip on the North Express fifteen years ago.

It had been in November; with brandy from a flask, Father cleared a small space through which I looked at the Astrakhan clad-and-booted guard up to his knees in snow. The sparks from the locomotive flashed above his head on a night wind lashing at his coat.

On my return to Longues I was packed off once again to Paris, but this time on the train, to secure tickets through the agency of the wonderful Mr. Wynn and his ubiquitous factotum Felix of the Travel Department at Morgan's. The best accommodation to be had on the *S. S. Manhattan* consisted in one single cabin in which the three of us, Mother and Father and I, should be together. We considered ourselves lucky at that, or rather Felix did.

Arrangements were made that we might stop at the Texas oil plant situated on Bec-d'Ambés, an island at the mouth of the Garonne, since no rooms were to be had at the hotels of Bordeaux and Biarritz.

I had traveled by train to Paris and was obliged to return by the same means to Longues and the family—this prior to driving to Bordeaux from Normandy. I had been alone in a compartment on the trip down from the country, but conditions proved different in leaving the capital: to be certain of a place on the train, I must send Roger, the chasseur of the hotel, to the station one hour ahead of train time.

In the crowded compartment, where Roger not without difficulty had deposited my bag, sat an old lady. She was very charming and within the hour ventured to inform me she lived at Tilly, near Mantes. I have kept the card she gave me; smiling delicately she sought it in a sewing bag where I might see a revolver lying amongst her wool and needles. Opposite us erectly sat a Polish peasant woman with two children clasped in her lap. As I restored her wretched bundles fallen from the rack, she told us in halting French her husband was in Poland, that she had been sent to some outlying town by the French Government.... The children bawled mercilessly. There were no separate classes on this train which was to take twelve hours instead of the usual three and a half, since trains for civilians were shunted to one side as the grinning, sweating, military Pinnard clattered by, their feet hanging from the open doors of freight cars and perched on the limbers of seventy-fives tarpaulined on flat cars. In June, I was to see the Senegalese on the limbers of their guns retreating in the brazen light of fire, the sky a blue glare from parachute flares. But now they were happy and I envied them the fulfillment of going to battle, or so I thought.

Soon the kind old lady descended, and a drunken Frenchman, drenched in tears at leaving his wife to proceed to Brest and the Navy, ascended; I retreated behind a book. At every station including Bayeux, soldiery were painting out the name of the town in watery and translucent paint. What idiocy to so attempt to disguise implacable identity. And then we left our dear Abbaye.

I was loath to leave France but since I had no reason to stay, I left as one leaves a new grave. The Embassy at Paris by circulars and by advertisements in the *Herald* had advised all Americans to return to the United States did they not have urgent reason to stay. I had hoped to serve as private secretary to Ambassador Hugh Wilson at Berlin but since he was recalled for a "consultation," perhaps the greatest blunder of our foreign policy in recent years, my job had lost significance. I had no choice but to leave.

At Tours I spent the night with friends. At their château I retired to a chintzed room where young girls of my acquaintance had lived who had once come to lovely Tourraine to receive a proper foreign lacquer and polish. At two in the morning, unable to sleep, I arose and went to walk in the forests of Chambord. In such a way I had walked with Fido in the moonlight, in the brown and blue night of Longues before I had left Normandy. I remember his face as lit up in the flame of his lighting a cigarette, and he had said, "It is finished," and threw the dead match away with finality. All about me wept the forests of Tourraine.

The next morning, I proceeded South and, near Bordeaux, stopped in a village and asked the road to the Texas refinery. I was directed on my way, but evidently impressed the fellow with whom I had spoken as suspect, for on arriving at Bec-d'Ambés, I was informed the refinery guards had been telephoned a suspicious individual in a low black car was headed in their direction, doubtless with evil intentions and a bomb in the back seat. It was all very new.

The family had presented the Commerciale to the Red Cross and were expected on the train. The Consul at Bordeaux treated with pompous detachment and inefficiency the countless Americans milling about seeking explicit information on the various subjects of their worries and discomforts or needs. Diplomacy, even consular, is essentially of personal relationships, and to large degree the men occupying the minor posts in our diplomatic service are incapable of establishing themselves in the countries to which they are sent. They are chosen for their intense Americanism and are sought at the geographical heart of our country, but to be too intensely of any nationality automatically inhibits one's efficacy in associating with those of different habits.

Soon we had rooms at the Splendide Hôtel and whiled away our time as best we could visiting the rock chapel of St. Emilion, observing the refugee children who seemed parentless and everywhere. A woman of the village told Mother the Army had taken her man while another who owned a neat macaroon shop interrupted her to say with a bang on the counter which shook the brazen scales, "That is nothing! They send us these dirty refugees with their diseases. Our children will all die—my Jeannot already has the pain of the ears…"

And sitting on the hotel terrace. Here we chatted casually with many as one will in the relaxation of aimless waiting, but I remember particularly Mr. Schmidt, President of the Chase Bank of Paris, who told us much of the bank bomb shelter which he averred was painted in white and contained a bar, bridge tables and like comforts. That it was utilitarian despite these fripperies was evident since on ascending from the *abri* after an alert, a piece of anti-aircraft shell was found by a teller in front of his cage. It had crashed through the skylight.

Bordeaux was blacked out. There was nothing much to do save to eat at various restaurants such as the Chapon Fin at which Edward the VII had ordered installed a special suite to be near that gourmet's paradise. It was in the rococo caverns of the restaurant that I remet Frank Griswold of Philadelphia and his lovely wife, Louisa. I say remet, since he had been a few years ahead of me at St. Paul's, and we were to have a wonderful time home on the *Manhattan* together.

They were placed in separate cabins; Frank with five individuals who played poker all the night with cigars in their mouths, flanked with bottles of whiskey, and Louisa was incarcerated with five women whose fare was brandy, and who, on undressing, festooned the berths and ventilators with their clothes. These individuals were respectively dubbed "The Boys" and "The Girls."

Finding it impossible to sleep in his cabin, Frank spent the first two nights on the top deck in a deck chair cheek by jowl with fuming Toscanini who none-the-less on arrival, I noted in the papers, expressed himself as having had an enjoyable voyage. Later it was rumored three feminine admirers had given up their cabin to the virtuoso. He might have ascended to those transcendental planes to which he leads his ready listeners, disdained discomfort and not have been so grumpy as Frank reported him.

Yet the meekness assumed by the Americans who traveled under these degrading conditions baffles me. In the writing room which was partitioned off to accommodate men passengers in cots, I saw much insubordination. A steward stood and laughed over a seasick passenger too weak to rise and since the steward did not help him, he was sick by his cot, to his own and everyone else's great discomfort. Another steward accosted Louisa and said, "Hello baby!" at which Louisa laughed and Frank was properly indignant.

"Grisvold, that's a good Cherman name," said Frank's steward to him approvingly one day. Half the crew it seemed were "German-

Americans," speaking German amongst themselves. Our steward, who was Irish, confided the German members of the crew being in the majority made it very unpleasant for the others below decks. The same conditions prevailed in July, 1940, when I returned for the last time, yet those whose sympathies are with the Nazis pass through the Panama Canal and are permitted to man our largest ships for they possess American passports.

Lord Beaverbrook was aboard and I found him much smaller than I had believed possible and very wrinkled with a simian face and I did not pay the attention I should now have wished to his conversation. He was rumored to be on an inspection tour of Canadian holdings.

Mr. William V. C. Ruxton was planning his now justly famous Ambulance Corps and was kind enough to show me his plans of campaign which are proving so immensely efficient. On arriving at New York he had not been on the dock five minutes before he received a subscription of $5,000. His plan was as joint master of the Quorn to appeal to the M. F. H.'s throughout the country. I considered applying as a driver, and Mr. Ruxton asked me to draw up a questionnaire to which all applicants should submit. I worked over one, including such items as "previous experience? languages? medical knowledge?" and presented it to him. At the end of my list, Mr. Ruxton appended "clubs?"

I saw him three months later at the American Hospital at Neuilly. He had collected $100,000, and was having some difficulty with the British Government as to how the money was to be spent. His achievement in those phlegmatic non-intervention days was unconscionable.

Toward the end of the voyage, the ship's stores ran out almost completely and on the last morning the steward said to my father who was salting his porridge, "You had better save that for your eggs, sir, it is all we have."

At last, sick at heart, we arrived in America; disheveled and vaguely resentful of American aplomb and lack of interest in the war, a sickness for all we felt to be forever left behind, a resentment for the assumption of superiority in America; an attitude we felt to be unjust in view of the suffering and courage we had witnessed. A lack of interest met with the expression of our grief which we would have tolerated had we not believed that grief for the tragedy of war must be shared by every one. Every man had two countries, his own and France, though this maxim would apply only to the Germans today. I was determined to return to my stricken love, my second land.

New York seemed heartless as always, but I was no longer impressed with her and thought her merely callous and without design and her lights far too bright after blackout Europe. She wore a whore's jewels and not the lights of a justified freedom.

I spent a miserable three weeks in Chicago doing everything in my power to become attached in some way to the Embassy at Paris, to affiliate myself with some concern having offices in that capital which I felt to be the axis of the world and, besides, the one place where I might continue to write a novel I had begun with furrowing brow a year before. It is not strange that artists and vague minds have gravitated to Paris for in her graygreen light one's spirit is unbound and she will let it soar up or down or in whatever direction it may take its flight and look the other way. Paris has so many jewels in her coffers she does not care for more though, like Thais, she exacts the love and presents of extremes in men. Like her daughters who wait in the cafés she cares little for sentiment and ideals and does not inhibit them, but perhaps in France this lack of interest in idealism, of taking it for granted, was carried too far. But now the pendulum has swung back, and they sing the *Marseillaise* with fervor at Cannes where before they could do little more than mumble the tune, while in America people are selling American flags and the churches are filling up and the men of God preaching war.

The heart and the mind urged me to Paris, and one day my brother said that Paul Mowrer, the editor of the *Chicago Daily*

News, had spoken to him casually about needing another man in Holland to study communications. My brother immediately—and for this I am and shall be eternally grateful—suggested me.

My father had been treasurer for Colonel, later Secretary of the Navy, Knox, the publisher of the paper, when he had made his run for the Vice-Presidency and together with Mr. Mowrer's kindness and some slight experience I had on the *Yale Daily News* while at New Haven, reason enough was found to give me the job.

In high spirits I reserved a berth on the Clipper, then an adventurous undertaking, though it is boarded like a street car today, purchased a money-belt, heavy shoes, airplane luggage and after a party to bid me farewell, at which a lady speaking from her then recent experience, advised me to take sleeping pills to dose myself with on the Clipper, I departed for New York to study the problem of cheapening communications and to familiarize myself with cablese.

I questioned everyone as to how in their opinion communications could be cheapened, but everyone was vague upon the issue and in Europe I discovered why—Mr. Huot of Press Wireless who headed the cooperative communication syndicate in Paris, of which the *Daily News* was a charter member, told me he kept a slide rule in his pocket with which to compute the various prices, since telegraph, teletype and telephone charges were for the most part established in terms of gold as the result of an international agreement arrived at in Geneva. For countries not on the gold standard, of which the currencies fluctuated daily, the prices must be translated into terms of gold: thus for communications in France, one paid in gold francs, despite the fact France was quite evidently not on the gold standard—a most confusing system but the best and only one possible under then extant conditions, for it was necessary in order to achieve a modicum of fluency that some common agreement as to charges between countries be arrived at.

Had the correspondents used but one of the four methods of communications, the matter would have been simplicity itself, but

The Pan Am Clipper, 1939

they switched from one to the other and as often as not used combinations of the telephone, telegraph, teletype, and the lowly letter. Correspondents used those methods which they found most practicable and left Huot to figure out the bill. What advice on economy he gave them was often disregarded out of their urgency. It is to Mr. Huot's everlasting credit that he achieved a paradox in keeping an open wire via Holland from Paris to Berlin during the greater part of the war. His conversations were of necessity oblique to the point of obscurity, since the line was trebly censored, yet he derived much from an intonation, an inflection.

Cablese is an absurd jargon permitted by the cable companies to journalists in order to reduce the number of words used in cable texts. It is fortunately quasiobsolete as the result of such cooperative, purely journalistic cable companies as Press Wireless which operate on a non-profit basis with but little overhead. The grammarians may stir with relief at the increasing excommunication of this unlovely synthesis, what Arnold Bennett (I believe) termed "the cacophony of journalism." Yet such papers as the *New York Times* have achieved a literary as well as journalistic conscience.

In New York, I watched the messages coming in, and an occasional dispatch in cablese being rearranged so as to make sense, thus implying the possibility of error. Having got wind of a Rome-New York telephone I called on Mr. Sulzburger of the *Times* in his immensely impressive offices crammed with mementoes of the stirring past of journalism and asked him if he would be kind enough to tell me about it. He replied that he knew nothing of such a telephone and very kindly called his foreign communications man who also stated he knew nothing.

Since that date a Rome-New York telephone is used by the *Times.* I understand the instrument is like a dictaphone; the message is pretalked on to a cylinder and the correspondent may listen to his dispatch before relaying it on the telephone without hesitations or valuable losses in time.

My Clipper was three days late, a very pleasant period for me spent at various feasts and the like and having tea at the Museum of Modern Art. Modern "art" which alone has prophesied the chaos of the future is a virulent agent of pessimism, merely mirroring the tragic deficiencies of our period, our lack of ideas, for it does not point at reform, but by its intimations, its esotericisms, tips us into a chaos and farther from basic truths explicit in nature. It is inherent in an artist to be an extremist since he must sense what his period lacks and make himself unpopular with some by the counsel of his art—as the doctor who gives medicine or the statesman who institutes reform. Yet Picasso and his ilk, the cubists, and the craftsmen, are false councilors and nihilists, in philosophy. It is not without significance Picasso has termed democratic art a lie; not without significance Hitler has banned free art from the Reich.

At last the day of flight came. I dutifully took bromides and turned my eyes up and to the East.

WAR: ANDANTE

MOTHER AND FATHER,

The flight to Bermuda was unpleasantly rough, and for the most part we squirmed uneasily in our seats. One half-hour previous to our arrival, we were forced to draw the little green blinds over the ports for we were in the British 'war zone"—many of us peeked, however, and the ice having been broken by a common dislike of the weather, we discussed what we should do in the event that we sighted a German submarine.

At Bermuda, I was much cheered by receiving your cable—the air of the island was *embaumé* and warm and welcome after the confinement we had suffered.

From Bermuda on, we were but half the number flying from New York.

The strata of air were calm, the clouds at times engulfing us, at others far below. It was cold and the *raum, raum* of the motors incessant.

I settled down at a table with Ronald Tree, M. P., a Dr. Reichman, who is Polish, and a third, a tea-taster by profession. The first two were carrying the pouches for their respective governments; Tree, his in a canvas bag stamped all over with various official markings, while the Polish secrets were padlocked into a voluminous briefcase. Both bag and briefcase were always in evidence and never beyond reach of their couriers—I am now convinced that Oppenheim's descriptions are genuine and shall no longer consider them ludicrous.

The tea-taster, a garrulous Welshman, regaled us with various anecdotes pertinent to his profession; he stated he did not drink or smoke since he could not afford to risk brutalizing his taste buds. He seemed more subjective about his particular sensitivity than a coloratura. We listened, our ears attuned to the bourdon of the motors, our attention but half given, the story but half told.

Soon I retreated to the stern cabin. The ports are so placed in the curving hull as to permit one to look directly down at the sea, and in the darkness of the cabin as we rushed through the night, I was made conscious of my solitude—of the vaporous sky above; of the cloudshrouded sea rolling its immensity on a spinning world below, the clouds and air and moon which we examine so casually when on the ground seemed quite without warmth now that I was so near.

What if we should fall? With a mighty ripping the tail tear off and I tumble through cold air to the venous sea…?

With this happy thought I gulped a sleeping potion and retreated to my berth and commenced to gyrate uncomfortably in a manner known to all those who undress behind the buttony green curtains of a Pullman berth. The latter was, however, much larger than that on a train.

I awoke at seven to see the familiar Azores through the port. There was a continuous confusion throughout the trip as to the time, for it seemed that every five minutes one must set back one's watch an hour. One passenger claimed that he commenced to eat at one and finished at ten in the morning. We all agreed that it was frightfully bad for the digestion, for in a manner of speaking, dessert preceded the entremets, digestion ingurgitation, but I shall go no farther.

But to return to the Azores; on landing, the teataster whom I shall designate henceforth as "T.T.," Tree, to be known as "M.P.," and I, to be known as "I," went for a ride in a car of unknown vintage and make, which we agreed might have been manufactured by the inexpert islanders from objects washed up on the beach.

We ascended a prominence, gaining a fine prospect of the green cones of mountains rising directly from the sea. I remembered my French professor and wondered if he had really done as he had promised himself he would—come to live on these temperate islands—to walk among the eucalyptus trees and in the fields in which boys pound tin pans all day and seem somnolently happy in spending their days as living scarecrows. Or perhaps he was on the little Azore on which lived the fabled Perfect Society undisturbed in their appropriately temperate Utopia.

We returned to the town, and there had a glass of hot chocolate while Portuguese youths applied themselves to the task of doing my shoes. The clever fellows inserted triangular leather patches into my shoe tops at either side of my foot to avoid getting the blacking on my stockings. By now we were told to return to the Clipper, and the four of us, T.T., M.P., I, and Pouch—for it had by now become a definite personality, having precedence through doors and sitting as a fourth at bridge—clambered into the taxi. The engine clanked, the fenders beat like wings and off we jolted to the tender; through ultramarine to the Clipper—a diapason of motors, a rush of water, a breathless jerk and clear.

A hot lunch.

"And there is Estoril to the left," the steward pointed.

And so it was; a beautiful landing which we commented on in offhand fashion, for we did consider ourselves experts by now.

Across a long gangplank I walked to Europe—I was no longer between two worlds, no longer aloof, no longer at one with the purity of clouds and the moon.

I must cope with Portuguese customs officials; I must retrieve my camera from a sealed English sack, I must, I must, I must.

"No, what? No cigarillos, pas d'armes á feu, si Senor, danke sheun—"

"O, qu' ai-je dis? —c'est la gaffe."

And now what is· this brown envelope, a cable on strange paper but the words are familiar and warm, they are "Good luck! Mary"—*which* Mary?

The night was spent at the Aviz—an excellent hotel, which had once been an *hôtel particulier* of an English Lord. It was the type of place where one floats in the bathtub while a gargantuan towel assumes a pleasant temperature over a specially contrived rack.

I dined with a friend and the Pole and his pouch. The latter had an unpleasant personality, unlike that of its English colleague, which I ascribed to its leathery countenance. We had a Portuguese wine with our pheasant. It was light and sweet, and then a rare vintage port with our dessert.

The Pole to bed with his pouch, the other gentleman and I to Estoril and the Casino…and what should it be but like the one at any little French town complete with a permanent film of Pearl White and German short subjects with sub-titles in Portuguese.

At the bar I entered into an exchange of words with a familiar type. He speaks several languages, all badly, and has a superb knack of getting on with chauffeurs, barmen and the like… he eventually becomes a concierge in a reputable hotel and continues his activities under the aegis of respectability.

In the words of my companion—

"I sucked that orange dry" for by the time I had got through chatting with him he had told us that we had come to the wrong establishment, that our taxi had charged us too much; he agreed to and was successful in dissuading the driver from asking 170 escudos for the trip rather than the conventional 100. Back to Lisbon, and after hesitation, to bed.

The next day we boarded our train. The journey was uneventful save for the fact that the Pole at dinner did me the compliment of slipping me his card with words scribbled on the reverse, cautioning me to discuss "nothing important" insomuch as he suspected a man near us of being a Rumanian spy. For the next few minutes I toyed with platitudes and an unpalatable chop immersed in Portuguese gravy.

The air was draughty with the flapping of spies' ears.

I seemed to recognize the waiters, but realized that I had seen their swarthy chins and burning black eyes on canvases by Goya, "El Greco," and Velasquez. I was different from them as are green and red, yet are not green and red both colors?

Through Spain we slept, yet we were *brusqués* and searched at both frontiers. San Sebastian was pitted with shell holes and eyeless houses stared at us as we passed.

Operations at the frontier were interminable as is this missive—I walked across the bridge between Spain and France, a bag in either hand. I taxied to Biarritz, looked for Vallombrosa who was not there, had a shave and a late lunch, and tea at a shop frequented by the Marquis of Cavadonga, a whisp of a mummy of a man, who it appears, plots endlessly over *brioche* and coffee with less exalted confederates for the Restoration in Spain.

From Biarritz to Paris, the trip was delightful—I shared my cabin with the "Rumanian spy," and glad I was of it for, as a French ore expert he was met at the station by a requisitioned car and chauffeur. He graciously offered me a lift, and I left my less fortunate friends standing on the quai. In the rain and darkness at 6:30 in the morning we splashed to the Ritz.

Paris with its muted lights is a city of fifty years ago. One does not think less of a friend because she is in mourning. To the contrary…

Yes, Paris was indeed gloomy and deserted. The work of evacuation had been only too well done and the city gray as the tomb stretched out emptily on every side. I felt my return somehow anticlimactic.

The Cambon side of the hotel was shut, and I had my choice of a room on the Place Vendôme or the garden. I chose the latter;

and having slept and rested, I set out into the gloomy streets with my camera.

The great majority of the shops were open and their windows which had been so hastily taped in September had now achieved a certain finesse—particularly the toy shops among the best of which was the wondrous Nain Bleu opposite the basilica dedicated to the use of the Polish refugees in the rue St-Honoré. It was at this shop my father had purchased a battleship model to present to King Michael of Rumania. My parents I remember had first considered hiding it so that I should not have the disappointment inherent in seeing and not receiving such a magnificent present—yet they thought better of it and I felt self-righteous and martyric when it was carried from the house in a specially contrived crate.

After the young King was told how to work the ship, his mother, Princess Helen, admonished him not to forget the intricate windings of the clockwork which pivoted turrets and motors, whereupon he turned and said with great composure, "I never forget," bowed and departed to his nursery. Certainly he admitted to a trait unfortunate in a central European monarch.

The Nain Bleu windows were decorated with a Don Quixote in blue tape laying his lance above a shield emblazoned in swastikas at a windmill of the same color. These pictures done in colored and sometimes transparent papers I photographed and sent home where they were reproduced in *Townsfolk*, a Chicago magazine—which I later learned neatly scooped *Life* by two days in reproducing my photographs with a sonorous explanation.

Various shops in Chicago copied these criss-crossings of gummed paper to attract attention likewise.

After calling on friends who were for the most part away, I gave up in despair when Major Guichard, resplendent in his navy-blue uniform and gold braid, gave signs of life, and we had lunch together in the desolate dining room of the hotel. Over a meal which was not in the least an evidence of war, Major Guichard informed me that he was charged with the inspection and check of aviation

Famous toy store Au Nain Bleu prepared for war

supplies and asked me to accompany him on his tours, though he said, with a laugh, it was dangerous work since a month before he had a collision with another car in the utter darkness of the roads behind the Line. He had suffered a broken arm and nose, while his chauffeur was stripped of his trousers and drove the Major to the hospital in that condition. Monsieur Guichard said he was so amused at seeing his chauffeur blushing with a bare posterior that he quite forgot to feel pain.

I regret that I never went on an inspection with the Major, but I doubt if even he were conscious of scarcity; at least he never appeared worried.

Mandel was seated in his corner of the dining room with his famous blonde mistress. "Quand Clemenceau pet, c'est Mandel qui pu" was the World War I maxim, and the barber at the Ritz supplemented the extraordinary relationship implied in the above by saying Mandel was Clemenceau's son by a Rothschild. The good coiffeur went every morning to Mandel's apartment in the Avenue Victor Hugo to shave him and said the Minister's rooms were lined with photographs of the Tiger—but that is not surprising, considering their close association. I never did discover who Mandel was though there were many theories. Yet all agreed to the fact that he was the most efficient man in the Cabinet. Later, when he acceded to the Portfolio of the Interior, all felt the hot weight of his glare as it shifted to France from the colonies he had directed so well.

Toward the close of our luncheon, Major Guichard advised me to give the head waiter a tip which seemed to me preposterous but I did so with as good grace as possible. I was well rewarded for whenever I lunched or dined thereafter either at Ciro's or the Ritz I infallibly appeared in the columns of the *Herald* the next morning as having been with such and such reigning prince, general or cabinet minister. There was no one I did not know. My acquaintances were secretly impressed and I thought it very funny and was occasionally embarrassed. I did get a table whenever I wanted one, for the restaurants were soon to become crowded as of yore, and I was directed to it by the maître d'hotel himself with a flourish, a signal honor, for which I was continuously and duly appreciative though I would sometimes groan secretly at the heavy tax of a *noblesse oblige* which the Major had imposed upon my slender resources.

On my reporting to Mr. Edgar Mowrer, brother of Mr. Paul Mowrer, he presented me to my associates, Paul Ghali, a charming Egyptian, most conversant with the intricacies of the Quai d'Orsay, the various ministries and embassies, and to Mike Taylor in charge of the business end of the office. Since there was virtually no news, Mr. Mowrer gave me a week to find an apartment and settle generally and advised me what papers to read and of the general routine of the office.

Mr. Mowrer is an astonishing man and it was a great pleasure to work under him. His thoughts moved with such rapidity and were so little betrayed by his face that he was a difficult man to converse with when he was not the conversational aggressor. After mentally sifting evidence, it was his habit to sit at his typewriter and with an incredible rapidity type out his brilliant articles without using the punctuation or capitalization keys. Prone to editorializing, or journalistic prophecy, he suffered the trials and tribulations of prophets. Though journalists speak with deep admiration of his analysis of the cause of the Reichstag fire which he observed despite a broken leg, I have heard him called with some sarcasm, "a-million-thoughts-a-minute." Certainly no man who had anything to do with him could feel indifferently about Mr. Mowrer.

Through the kind offices of the Misses Benedict of the Benedict Bureau I found just the apartment I sought at number 81 Avenue Victor Hugo—this after examining some five or six flats on the Ile St. Louis, in the Faubourg St. Germain, Faubourg St. Honoré, and, as a last resort, below the Tour d'Argent, for the restaurant of renowned ducks boasted several apartments under the same management. There at lunch I sat alone overlooking the Seine flowing through the wet empty grayness of Paris, and was approached by a young aviator. He was the son of the patron, and when I mentioned that I was looking for a flat he showed me around to ones I considered too big for myself alone, but at a sign from him, and as an inducement, ten per cent was removed from my check. He had the manners of a prestidigitator. Later I was to visit Ghali in one of these apartments which he conveniently shared with a young lieutenant occupying a minor post in the cabinet of a member of the General Staff. I told him of the aviator who had showed me about: "Oh him—*he's un aviateur de terre*, an aviator of the ground," said Paul with scorn. And I remembered the aviator showing me his identification bracelet. Pierced with little holes at the center, his name was reproduced on either half and the bracelet was a silver reproduction of those used by the ordinary soldiers. "If one is killed, the bracelet is split in two, one segment to be nailed to one's forehead, the other to be sent to one's *bonne amie*," he winked. Later, Cartier got out identification bracelets in gold and wood and called them the "touch wood—for luck" bracelets.

Map of Paris from the late 1930s with places significant to Peter of particular note:

- 80 Place de Victor Hugo - Peter's apartment
- Rue Raynouard, Adrian Goekoop's apartment
- Hôtel de Crillon - home of the Crillon Grill - a lunch place

- The Ritz - where Peter often went for tea at Lady Rendl's suite
- Hôtel Continental - home of Press Wireless
- Rue de Vaugirard - The Chambrun residence
- Hôtel Regina - where Peter met with Polish officials
- Shéhérazade and Casino de Paris - haunts that Peter frequented

Place Vendôme with sand bags protecting the base of the monument to Napoleon, Paris, 1939

It is difficult to convey the dreariness of Paris, virtually a dead city, and the weather was incessantly gray with the clouds low over the spires, cupolas and smokeless chimneys of the metropolis.

Soon I was settled in my apartment. It was situated in a pavilion, on the second floor, and had a balcony on the inner court of the apartment house. The walls were covered with bad but fortunately obscure eighteenth century paintings of ladies and gentlemen in presentable frames. The ceiling was very high and in the slanting Mansard roof above the French window leading out onto a balcony had been pierced a "studio window" or large skylight. The furniture was all Louis XV or XVI with a voluted Empire day bed on which I slept. It was all very pleasant and suitable, the large bathroom, salon-bedroom and small ante-chamber with its yellow walls and Toulouse-Lautrec prints and brass receptacle for my umbrella and the large fireplace I might sit before.

I procured the services of a maid for 300 francs a month after first making a stab at using Roger, the nineteen-year-old chasseur of the France et Choiseul Hôtel which had closed as most hotels save the Ritz, the Meurice and the Crillon. He proved inefficient and more of a liability than a convenience, and soon he secured a job in a restaurant and I saw him no more. Not so Fanny the maid who was wonderful. For 300 francs a month she did the apartment and my clothes and blacked my shoes better than they've ever been done before or since. Her husband was mobilized though he had one finger missing, lost in some misadventure of his trade which was that of baker. Fanny said he was stationed as a guard near a mustard gas factory in Picardy. At first Fanny made me my matutinal chocolate, but as I had to be ready when the chocolate was, I finally gave up and had it at the bistro in the Place Victor Hugo before going to work; yet I was sorry since it had been Fanny's habit to listen to the dawn radio news broadcast and regale me with information as she cooked breakfast.

Having stocked the apartment with firewood, a maid and other necessities, as well as having subscribed to ten newspapers: the Leftist *Le Populaire*, the Left-Liberal *L'Oeuvre*, the pro-Government *Petit Parisien*, the Rightist-Catholic *Figaro*, the Military-Nationalist-Rightist *Epoque*, the ex-pro-German *Matin*, three English papers, and the *Paris Herald Tribune*, I found I had much of my week left and decided to visit my friends near Besançon.

(Later I discovered that though there existed an appreciable difference in the point of view of the English papers, the French papers differed in nothing save headlines and featured articles. I abandoned them all in disgust and read only the *Herald Tribune*, far more instructive than all the others since it often carried items the others did not. For some reason the censors were more lenient with it, and I ended by keeping all the French papers folded and unopened. One day I should use them in place of the firewood.)

Paul Ghali had warned me that I had better not present myself at the Hôtel Continental, headquarters of the Information and Bureau de Presse until I was quite certain what sort of identification papers and permits I should want. All the enlarged Government bureaus were in hotels. When it was discovered much of the stock of these last were owned by politicians, new buildings were hastily constructed. The public did not of course hear much of it. With a controlled press in wartime, a politician with bad instincts is uninhibited. As I was later told in America by an editor of the *Figaro*, "The Press did not play a pretty rôle in France."

Having impressive letters in suitably large envelopes to Daladier and the French customs, I was determined, on the literal weight of these to go into the military zone where lay Besançon. I visited the local gendarmerie. The gendarmes were politely impressed but stated they could not supply me with appropriate documents in less than three weeks, since my past must first be subjected to an "inquest." The endless scribbling with purple ink and thin pens, the *paperasse*, the hecatombs and catacombs of pink, white, yellow, gray, and black papers filled out in handwriting as illegible as the checks one got at restaurants; these seas of documentation of the Hôtel-de-Ville in which the French were buried up to their noses, were mazes into which the enemy easily found his way. Much later, after kicking my heels endlessly on various commissions, I decided to single out one woman of ancient vintage to whom I sent boxes of candy in return for expeditious governmental service. By such simple expedients I never thereafter stood in line.

Each Ministry of the Government and each Bureau of the Military, jealous of its prerogative, was in a position to issue a permit of circulation. Later it became obvious to me that in many cases the examiners were unfamiliar with the form of the document they were examining. At first scrupulous in procuring papers—a lengthy operation—I later, in common with many honest Frenchmen and others less honest, developed a scorn for the examiners and traveled everywhere on the strength of my *laissez-passer* which was as often as not unexamined and my American passport which commanded considerable respect everywhere. Should America go to war, every citizen should be issued a passport with his fingerprinted photograph attached and the visa pages be dedicated to travel permissions beyond limits specified on a consideration of his duties.

A bit discouraged at my rebuff and unwilling to wait for an inquest into my past, I went to call on Captain Edmond Spitzer who was on the staff of the Fourth Military Bureau at the Invalides. He invited me to lunch with him at the restaurant on the Quai des Grands-Augustins where the bold pirate Lapérouse warped his ship. From the window of the little room we looked out on the sky, the Seine and old stones and had two dozen *marennes* apiece with lemons and vinegar and the specialty, a duck *éspiégle* and mushrooms *follette* with a Chambertin 1906, and Calvados "*fine du prêtre*" with our cigars. Monsieur Spitzer, who in peace time was Director General of the Franco-Polish Bank, had influence in the correct quarters sufficient to get me the papers I wished and that evening I bought my ticket at the wet and smoky Gare de l'Est for Besançon; and soon in my second-class carriage I watched the leaden hues of the devolving twilit scenery, the dripping telegraph poles flicking by to the clickety-click and felt the singing bounce of a European railway car. Soon I slept, to awake in utter darkness intensified by the small blue light allowed by regulation in our compartment. The people were huddled in their seats motionless and swathed as the mummies in catacombs. On we bounced through the night flicking past the blue light of stations, occasionally stopping amidst the shouts and roughness and smell of the soldiers, their bottles of pinard protruding from the musettes slung over their shoulders, their rough boots scraping over the puddled quais, through steam purling under the swathed glare of arc lights. It was strange this common assumption of secretiveness. All the trains were forever filled, the passageways jammed so that I must come hours before the train left, or send a chasseur to keep a place for me. People were not as yet used to war, and they had acquired the restless habit of useless movement.

On exuding from the padded coffin at Besançon, I bustled with the crowd to the exit to be stopped to have a policeman or gendarme perfunctorily examine my pink circulation slip in the wretched gaslight; then passed by my friend unseeing. I turned back with apologetic surprise at a pained little "hey!"

What a charming château it was, this familiar château near Besançon, so well proportioned, so exquisite in the perfection of detail, my nostrils were filled with the mixed and not unpleasant smells of aging wood and plaster and my eyes rested on age-attenuated colors and mottled mirrors acquiring such a pleasant grayness, not rude as the perfection of modern mirrors. Perhaps a comparison might be made; they are as candle light is to the electric light bulb, these old mirrors to the new. Yet we are beginning to reappreciate nuance with our blue glass and indirect lighting. We are the only ones who can afford nuance today. Everywhere else one must be without subtlety.

The windows were painted in calcimine from the inside and heavily shrouded with curtains as well. The château had known war, it had served as headquarters for Prussian divisions in 1870, and in the attic was a set of Empire furniture upholstered in green satin ornamented with wreathed "Ns" on which the German officers behaved like pigs. There are many stories of this first German occupation certainly no less rapid than Hitler's. A friend of mine in Tourraine had in his employ a gardener whom the villagers call "The German" because his mother, a village girl, had been seduced by the father, a Uhlan cavalryman, seventy years before.

It was quite cold and my cousin and I would go for long walks on the days she was not training to be a nurse at Besançon; or to the village where she supervised the knitting. I remember waiting for her in the bitterly cold little schoolroom of the mayor's house in which the women congregated to knit and I examined republican propaganda—a picture of serfs tugging at a plow while a lord with a coronetted helmet sat a caparisoned horse watching them scornfully at their labors. The picture was titled *La France sous les Rois*. Under another case were different sorts of grain, and further along bugs and parasites neatly parading on cardboard with pins stuck through them.

I had been presented to the ladies of the village once before, but had desisted from their company when my cousin had been smilingly asked with popped eyes and raised eyebrows in nodding heads if I were her *future.*

I became bored and went outside where I saw an old woman pass with a basket over her arm. In the distance we could hear the dull bam-pac of the D. C. A.[1] or anti-aircraft as the guns fired and shrapnel burst in two-step time, bam-pac, bam-pac. I raised my hat and we both looked up as a plane passed far over head in the cold blue sky. Her eyes were as clear and untroubled as she lowered them to mine.

"I know them well," she said. "I was nine when they came the first time and the marks of their spurs are all over the kitchen table yet… We called them Prussiens then, and now Boches, but they're still the same," she added with a shrug as she turned to hobble on her way.

I looked after her, and when she had turned into a little house I followed down the rutted frozen road and found a Nazi leaf on the road. This propaganda was the most effective I have seen. Cut in the form of a large leaf and stamped a dull brown, it bore on one side a skull in the crested French helmet and on the other in strange and prophetic verse:

"This Autumn, the leaves fall.

Next Spring, Frenchmen, you will fall as they."

At last the knitting was over and my cousin issued from the house with a crowd of women and then I showed her what I had found. She answered with a smile and closed her eyes as she nodded.

Apparently all sorts of things were found in the region: coffee that the English had thrown into Germany in little sacks, as blatant evidence of their own surplus, was dutifully returned by the Germans to the French with sarcastic notes attached, and it was reputed that explosive toys and poisoned candy were dropped as well and that a little boy in the "next village" had had his hand blown off by a mined doll. I attempted to find which village, but

1. Abbreviation for Défense Contre Avions.

never could, though I neither believe nor disbelieve the story for reasons which are today apparent.

In a field on the next estate, a rubber balloon containing a greenish liquid was discovered between two furrows. The farmer who had stumbled upon it believed it contained dread Hyperite, or mustard gas, and called the police who came and took it away, and did not return to satisfy local curiosity. Had the farmer been correct in his surmise, which is doubtful, the green fluid would have represented the first use of gas in the war though the Germans used it later in Belgium and Holland. The farmer appeared honest enough.

In the woods, my cousin was told by a *garde-forestier*, a huntsman too old for military service, that another parachute had been found. I asked to see the torn silk with its empty harness hanging from a branch.

The next day we had tea at the chateau of the Marquis de Scey, and a two-star general told of a captain who had been stopped on a road leading East by a gendarme who examined his papers, and after a careful perusal, saluted and let him pass. Casually, on arriving at the Line, the captain asked his superior officer if they were searching for someone, since he thought it surprising to have been stopped so nearby and told of his experience. Immediately suspicious, the superior officer answered, "I think we are," and, ordering a car, drove to the spot at which the captain had been stopped, there to find a gendarme's uniform rolled and thrown in the ditch.

"The parachutist," explained the brigadier, "had examined the papers of some ten officers before leaving—and of course he left with the knowledge of which regiments were stationed where."

Apparently the fellow had landed with a French uniform and a bicycle as well as a change of clothes, and if he had a German accent it wouldn't have mattered for almost everyone did speak in gutturals so near Germany, and doubtless he was equipped with more papers than the President of the Republic himself.

By such tactics, when President Lebrun visited the Line in

utmost secrecy, the German loudspeakers were able to bellow at him: "Bonjour, Monsieur le President." An experience doubtlessly disconcerting to lachrymose "Bébert."

Yet again a village boy had seen a "nun" shaving in the woods.

All this to show the life in the shadow of the Maginot Line. I wrote an article about it with great flourish and detail and later gave it to Mr. Mowrer on his return to America just before Christmas. He may have forgotten it in his pocket or considered it trivial, but I think at the period when everything was so dull my trivialities in experience might have proved more interesting than the political generalities that filled the press; all of which later proved to be laboriously censored error on the most important issues.

When I remember that from September, 1939, to June, 1940, the American public read nothing but flagrantly inaccurate and censored "news" it is a wonder to me that they still permit themselves to voice opinions on what is happening abroad. One simply cannot tell. Everything concerning France for those nine months of sit-war was censored balderdash. The newspapers were serviceable but for one thing.

Back in Paris, I took up my new duties. Hanging to the back of the autobus every day, I went down to the Place de l'Opéra where the offices were situated. Mr. Mowrer, Mr. Huot of Press Wireless, and Mike Taylor were convinced nothing much could be done to ameliorate the telegraph lines or the prices thereof, and rather than proceed to Amsterdam I remained in a Paris becoming more populous every day, so much so that a second evacuation would be required in June.

Back they came, and one by one the restaurants opened, the curfew was retarded from ten to twelve and, at Christmas, dancing and public music were permitted. My telephone jangled pleasantly, heralding friends back on leave, or returning to the capital after self-imposed rustication, seeking a gay time. My work was of the lightest and the most interesting imaginable since it consisted in the attempt to fill in the censored blanks of the newspapers from conversations I had overheard, from presumption, or as a last resort, intuition. I would mark in red, articles I deemed of particular interest and would submit them to Mr. Mowrer.

His invariable habit was to call the American Ambassador for confirmation of his own opinions which he seemed to pluck from the air. Paul Ghali, who was acquainted with all the *chefs de cabinet*, virtually undersecretaries of state, of the various ministers, as well as the ministers themselves, and their political colorings and natures, knew how to derive truth from their utterances. "The Minister is tired and probably pessimistic—things aren't so bad as he pictures them," or, "When the Minister is tired he tells the truth, or lies, or exaggerates." Paul was magnificent. Occasionally we went to the Continental to hear Monsieur de Laboulaye address the press, but his releases, supposedly the official and solitary oracle of news, were insufficient beyond belief and his conferences for the most part were attended by the correspondents merely to keep in the good graces of his department and the respect of the delightful Monsieur de Laboulaye who had been so justly popular in Washington as Ambassador.

One day I stepped upstairs from such a conference to see an old friend, Monsieur Laroche, who had been at Warsaw as French Ambassador and was then impressed into service as head of the Redaction, or editorship of releases to the press. On all sides in those long empty white corridors I heard the blind, clattering urgency of the teletypes. What can compare to the hammering restlessness of these machines? Their rhythm is that of the world today.

One morning, I entered the office to find Mr. Mowrer writing an article about price level enforcements. I was summarily directed to discover what was being done. Determined to do or die, I made a list of twenty necessities such as soap, potatoes, bread, meat of various kinds, etc., and set out to ask prices. Invariably, as the law imposed, they were the same everywhere, even at the little shops which had a down-at-heels and otherwise disreputable look. Finally at such a one I asked the patronne how the police checked on their wares.

"But, Monsieur, they come like you and ask!" I made the rounds again, purchasing rather than asking and got a divergent set of statistics (as well as assorted groceries) dissimilar in many ways from those imposed by decree in the *Journal Officiel.*

To cap off my list, I made an appointment with Monsieur Barthélemy, a neighbor of Normandy who was proficient in business and owned vast dairy interests. At the appointed hour, I was introduced into his office at the Halles, that noisy group of warehouses in whose interstices rumble drays laden high with odoriferous vegetables, noisy pigs and cows, where all the produce of the great city is assembled and sorted. He received me very kindly and gave me a magnificent collection of statistics on consumption, production and cost of butter, milk, cheese and eggs. I was most appreciative.

Madame Barthélemy, who framed herself in a lovely hôtel near the Etoile received every one of any importance in Paris. And many whose sole importance was that of being seen at Madame Barthélemy's. Always one encountered supercilious staff officers with their rows of orders and well polished nails and a minister or two. In other words, the Barthélemy's were in a position to be well informed, yet I remember in August Monsieur Barthélemy asserting with all the positiveness of the shrewd business man that German equipment was very inferior, "to such a point in fact that after the annexation of Austria the roads were littered with ersatz tanks and trucks which had broken down because of inefficient oil and materials; that in addition the German army is badly officered." He explained omnisciently that officers to the rank of lieutenant were passably trained as were the generals, but there was nothing worth mentioning between these extremes. Such propaganda was an infection the French caught inadvertently and conveyed to one another with the best intentions. The principle error was, "*They* most certainly have not enough petrol." Such a statement was the quietus to any argument purporting the efficiency of the German military machine, yet Ambassador Henri-Haye told me recently that when the Germans came into Versailles, he saw columns leave their engines idle as they had lunch at the various cafes of the Place.

Later I was instructed to discover what preparations the French were making for Christmas. I went to the Ile de la Cité where Christmas trees are sold and on the way suddenly noticed my taxi driver was a woman, "Aha," I noted, "here is a story. '*Eh bien*, how long have you been at this?'" I feinted.

"For fifteen years, Monsieur."

So as my life continued and settled to a certain routine, friends began to turn up and my afternoons and evenings were spent in going out with the younger attachés and officers and soldiers who might be *en permission*, and I noted in my Journal:

"...To careen through the night in an ill-lit taxi, jerking and coughing on inadequate war-fuel; to draw up abruptly at an entrance, unfamiliar and forbidding in the black-out; these experiences which have become routine, are the imposed hors-d'oeuvres to an evening's outing in Paris.

"Barely four months ago the glow of this *ville ténebréuse* was visible at a distance of fifty kilometers, lurid as the City of Death against the night, and now Parisian lampposts sport tin hats restricting light to a perimeter of visibility at their base; automobiles with dimmers an opaque blue, and no light shows at windows of the houses. After six it would be folly to venture abroad without one's papers and a flashlight.

"A select group which would seem to move fluidly from one capital to another, despite mazes of regulation, grown to alarming proportions sympathetically with Parisian bureaucracy, opines that Paris is not so dark as London where pedestrians find themselves reduced to following the blind; nor as blacked-out as Berlin where nothing is seen, and nothing heard after curfew save the S. S. guard as it tramps through echoing streets.

"Since the beginning of hostilities, one does not have meals served at home. Febrility and an innate desire to be at the 'center of things' force one to the public places which overflow with individuals possessing a purpose for remaining in Paris.

"Fraternity, a virtue which becomes a cult during war and revolution, is rampant. Everywhere may be found someone who 'knows,' everywhere is someone with whom to talk, for topics are not difficult to find.

"Young heroes, affluent and on leave dine at Maxim's in their *uniformes de fantaisie*, their boots, spurs, and swagger sticks; their monocles and new Croix de Guerre distinguishable from those of the previous war by a different arrangement of the scarlet and green stripes of the riband...

"Maxim's Naïads, who have disported themselves voluptuously on the walls of that unparalleled establishment for a half century forever unveiling before their dim painted lakes, smile on the young officers for they evoke a less disenchanted Paris, a way of life which Proust annotated in his melancholy, endless prose.

"In their Paquin bustles and *fouragéres*, the waltzers spin under the orange glass of the ceiling. The women's skin plays in chiaroscuro with the red plush of the settees. They move and smile and forget and nod to the chorded disconsonance of a Tzigan orchestra. An era is evoked; one senses the Paris of 1914, for Maxim's as the war, is an anachronism. Most certainly the young have never had such an opportunity to understand the old.

"Yet soon, the officers rise to leave, Abdul and Albert bow to the ground, the commissionaire whistles a taxi and off it bumps to a show.

"The Folies-Bergéres being closed, the Casino de Paris, with tawny Josephine Baker singing Carmen Miranda's songs in the first act, and Maurice Chevalier his own in the second, is having a vast non-competitive success. With keen patriotic zeal and commendable appreciation for the spirit of the *entente cordiale*, half the chorus are pleased to be British and the revue has been dubbed *Paris-Londres*.

Peter resting during a moment of *"drôle de guerre"* high life

"At eleven, the wise go to bed and the initiate gather at various bottle clubs, which have experienced a mushroom growth.

"Madam de B., bored by the regulated closing hour of all theaters, night clubs, cafes, etc., determined to receive her friends at her apartment. They in turn might bring whom they wished, provided a nominal sum is paid for whatever is consumed. Her husband is only too pleased with this invasion of his privacy, as are many other officers home on leave. One dances to a radio, or sips a drink, or chats amiably with strangers in uniform.

"And then out into the street, dark and cold, to find a cab and to remember that the war is on. The reality of war is sometimes felt at night, yet the dreadful potentialities are dormant, and so, *en attendant* one yawns..."

Mr. Leander McCormick-Goodhart of the British Embassy at Washington had been kind enough to give me a letter of presentation to a Sir Ronald Campbell at Paris, saying that he would write of me to this gentleman.

On arriving I was gratified to discover that the new British Ambassador at Paris was a Sir Ronald Campbell and departed happily to arrange my presentation through the Press Attaché, Sir Charles Mendl. After careful scrutiny by the commissionaire ("We've got to be careful these days, you know"), I was admitted to the inner courtyard and taken up a stairway to a waiting room overlooking the Faubourg St. Honoré. No sooner had I arrived than Sir Charles entered beaming under his magnificent mustachios and looking very much as might have the dapper Berry Wall twenty years ago. I presented myself, gave him the letter of presentation and explained that Mr. McCormick-Goodhart had written of me to the Ambassador. He shook his head and my hand, told me to return in two days if I would and that he should have arranged everything. So infectious was he that I almost ran down the stairway in sympathy with his tempo.

Two days later I returned, nothing was said about my letter, but I was asked to luncheon at Sir Charles' apartments on the Avenue Matignon. Since he was one of the great gourmets, I anticipated the meal considerably and was not disappointed.

I arrived at one to find the Hon. H. A. Hankey and his colleague McLean, both young attachés and another man of the "wavy-navy," as the Royal Navy reserves were called in consideration of the wavy gold braid on their sleeves. I stammer slightly, and Sir Charles, delighted to find a topic of conversation on which he might embark without effort permitting him the while to think of other things, his luncheon, the other guests and the cutlets grilling in the kitchen, delightedly presented me to every one as "the American who stammers." Later he presented me to his wife, Elsie de Wolff, as "a fella who stammers and writes books."

I immediately took to Hankey and we saw much of one another. In Portugal, in July, I ran into a member of the British Embassy; he told me Hankey had driven away from Paris on some mission the thirteenth of June and had not been heard of since. Of short stature with an alert face and keenly intellectual eyes, he was a fount of interesting though never indiscreet information and a true son of his father, Lord Hankey, of whom John Gunther has written in the following terms, "Consider for instance the indispensable quality of a man like (then) Sir Maurice Hankey whose very name is unknown to millions but who combines in his person the posts of Secretary to the Cabinet, Secretary to the Privy Council, Secretary to the Committee of Imperial Defense, (and) What is more… shadows behind shadows are continually in the course of training to take over their master's jobs after retirement." Such a "shadow" was my friend.

Often we saw one another at the Crillon Grill and as often he would come late, or rush off early to attend to sending of code dispatches and deciphering those received.

At Sir Charles', I had on my right a Baronne de Heeckeren. I noted that in contrast with her abetted beauty she wore her nails clipped and unpainted and asked her if she were an artist. She answered yes, that she was a violinist. The lady on my left later informed me Madame de Heeckeren had taken first prize at the Conservatory in Paris.

Sir Charles gathered about him in his bachelor apartments, which he continued to maintain after his marriage to Elsie de Wolff, men and women who were not only fashionable but could do or had done something…perhaps this would explain his attachment to his wife. Beyond Madame de Heeckeren was Hankey and beyond him, a wonderfully blonde and beautiful Mademoiselle de Lourmel. My admiration was evident and after luncheon Madame de Heeckeren, whose cousin she was, gave me her address, for they shared an apartment, and permission to call.

Later Mademoiselle de Lourmel was to tell me of the dick-dick, the jade-eyed tiger and the silky panther padding among the fronds of Cochin China where she had undergone a novitiate in a convent. At the last moment, she explained with a smile, she had decided that such a life was not for her. It was interesting for me to imagine her coming to such a conclusion in the Oriental night, perhaps conscious of the sinewy tigers brushing beneath her and between the bamboo stilts of the unconventional nunnery. The inconsistency of European women, perhaps evidence of too much civilization, gives them a fantasy, a discontent, and later a philosophy which few others possess.

A lady at the piano played some Mozart, her diamond rings glinting wonderfully over the ivory keys, and we listened thoughtfully, and for the greater part in an effort to suppress our rumblings and ruminating over Sir Charles' cuisine. Soon I thanked him and left, having quite forgotten to ask him of my appointment with the Ambassador.

Only much later, and quite by chance, did I discover that my letter had been to another Sir Ronald Campbell, a gentleman who had been stationed at Paris but was sent as Minister to Belgrade on the Ambassador Sir Ronald Campbell's arriving to take up his new post. Sir Charles had evidently realized something was amiss when the Ambassador was presented with a letter from Mr. Leander McCormick, whom he knew but slightly, addressed to "Dear Ronnie," and failed to remember having received any further communication concerning me. Sir Charles, perfect diplomat that he was, had not said anything to me about it, but merely given me such a good luncheon and so many new acquaintances, that memory was conveniently deadened.

One morning as I lay in bed gazing at my skylight, wondering how I might cheaply have the vast expanse covered with a large black curtain so that I might rid myself of all the hat boxes my landlady had placed over the lights to prevent their shining upward and through the window in violation of the law, the mail was brought in with my innumerable newspapers. I occupied myself half-heartedly with the pile before me, drearily thinking that I must do something, since even with the hat boxes, the light had been considered too much, and the guard had come up twice and threatened to fine me should he be forced to come up a third time. Actually, it was a question of principle which annoyed me. I resented paying the entire price of large black curtains and my landlady was completely unconcerned when I told her that I was forced to live like a mole with her arrangements. I flung my newspapers, carbon copies of one another, into the corner until I came to an envelope on which appeared an embossed coronet surmounted by four baronial balls. I ripped it open and was delighted to find that Lady Decies asked me to luncheon. I accepted with alacrity.

On turning to my *Herald Tribune* I saw inappropriately in the "Americans in Europe" column that Prince and Princess Charles and Isabelle Radziwill were stopping at the Ritz. I telephoned my friend the concierge and asked him to arrange for me to present my respects the same afternoon at five.

Prince and Princess Radziwill had managed to leave Poland through the intervention of Prince Chigi, Grand Master of the Knights of Malta, and it was said all her jewels had been saved by the Biddles, yet that afternoon as we passed a vitrine of jade in the gallery joining the Cambon to the Vendôme side, the lovely Princess stopped automatically, then sighed and continued, saying, "Once I possessed such things," then she smiled and her eyes focused and she spoke of the hospital she had directed in Warsaw during the worst of the bombings.

She said she wished to organize an ambulance unit of the Maltese Cross and asked me who I thought would be the best man to see in order to secure the necessary papers and formalities. I suggested General Denain, then head of the Franco-Polish mission, or his *chef de cabinet*, President Pierre Cathala, who had a captain's commission and more recently was the head of the censorship in the Pétain Government. Princess Radziwill then asked how I thought money might best be raised in America and I advised her to write of the matter to my father whom I felt sure would turn the matter over to the Knights of Malta in America, which he did on receiving her letter. Princess Radziwill intimated the Order might be officially grateful to, ah, hum, beneficiaries. I left, my mind in flames.

I had a very enjoyable time at Lady Decies'. A Mrs. Corey was there, remarkable for eating with her black gloves on, something at which the lady I was seated beside raised her eyebrows in disapprobation; Lady Monde ate her truffles in silence, her immense emerald and diamond solitaires occasionally knocking against the table. There would be heightening of the conversation to cover these interruptions as when an old gentleman belches at table. I was much questioned about Ambassador Bullitt concerning whom the French, who were not asked to his receptions, were most curious, particularly by a Monsieur Henri, a boor of a man with a bristly head and an uncouth voice. He had the Chevalier ribbons of the Legion of Honor and Polonia Restituta in his lapel and I was curious as to who he might be. A gentleman beside me whispered he was reputed to be the illegitimate son of Painlevé and much in vogue since he was presumed to have much power and inside information.

"He has entrée to Gamelin, but at any hour..."

French Politics are Machiavellian, for it was impossible to judge a man's political color—of which there existed a vast complexity of nuances—by his occupations, appearance or Government position. Their often obscure duties, from which many derived excessive power, presented a contrast with the American fondness for concise labels.

Jean Cabestan of the Quai d'Orsai, told me that Henri was the one man whom Sikorski, the Polish Premier, would receive day or night. "Même quand il est sur son pot de chambre." Jean Cabestan himself, though an old friend, wielded for me mysterious powers. Dr. de Martel, the renowned surgeon, who trepanned Cabestan seven times as the result of a fracture he had received from a fall during a stag hunt, stated Cabestan was the most intelligent man he had ever met. Of the hunt in which he suffered his accident, Jean told me he had served the stag brought to bay in the streets of Versailles. It was at the time of the Front Populaire and the sit-down strikes, and Monsieur Cabestan of the Quai d'Orsai must have been quite a sight as he dismounted from his horse with his top boots, doeskin trousers and sky-blue coat, to slay the stag with his sword before the hooting Communists who were disgusted at what they considered unnecessary cruelty to an inoffensive animal.

Dr. de Martel operated principally in the American Hospital. I say "operated" since it is well known that he could not tolerate the thought of Germans in Paris and blew out his immensely educated brains at his post. He was revered, and I remember being told at the American Hospital that he considered an appendix operation so trivial and boring that he insisted always that a colleague accompany him with whom he might converse while disdainfully removing such a minor organ.

But I have wandered, yet I shall not apologize for digressions against which my reader has been warned at the outset.

On my leaving, Lady Decies graciously asked me to return for dinner the next Saturday.

The next Friday, I accompanied Princess Radziwill to Lady Mendl's for tea-the object of wonder was Captain Holland of the much-sunk *Ark Royal.* I found Lady Mendl remarkable and I admired the row of her decorations and in particular one I distinguished to have a sable riband bearing a Maltese cross under her white lace. I wandered about a bit, had some champagne and soon left… On my departure I saw the fronds of the palms in their porcelain pots by the glass doors turning brown in the cold winds, the veneer on the cartouched and gilded walls crumbling to dust and the maîtres d'hotel seemed more men and less waiters. In this supremely trivial Paris which witnessed what might be the last of the remnants of the old order, I felt the columns might soon buckle, the fronds rot, and Lady Mendl's teas were held on an inclined plane down which France danced a scherzo to inevitable doom. I had very much the same sensations at the debutante parties I attended this year in America.

The same afternoon I had noted in my Journal:

"And again the cold has come to blight civilians and facilitate the armed passage of frozen canals and lakes.

"Yet despite the imminence of a paroxysm, life proceeds much as before. Governments and populations sit as parents at the bedside of the international situation, for their offspring has given symptoms of acute illness, yet since the child has been put to bed, subjected to a regimen of constant observation, there remains little to be done...with six million men under arms and the impedimenta of defense increasing.

"Unmobilized men go to their jobs in the morning and to their clubs in the evening and are occupied at all times of day with the details of their particular *oeuvre*, for charity and war-work take precedence over all things.

"Ladies do what ladies usually do in the morning, and in the afternoon attend knitting bees under the high auspices of Ladies Acheson and Doverdale, at which reunions it would appear the most fantastic rumors are given birth and sufficient stature to survive for a bit in the cold world without.

"The garrison of the Ritz consists of wasp-waisted and shiny-booted officers who appear with jinglings of spurs and military infallibility at the cocktail hour. Their commander is Major Phillips, one of the Duke of Windsor's old Etonian equerries (now stationed at Nassau) resplendent in the uniform of the Scots Guards."

At Lady Mendl's, I had intimated to Princess Radziwill that in my opinion Lady Decies might contribute to her *oeuvre*. The Princess, as a result of the unflagging efforts of the editor in charge of the "Americans in Europe" column of the *New York Herald Tribune*, knew I had been received by Lady Decies and countered by suggesting firmly that I be the one to solicit.

Soon after, I returned to Lady Decies' magnificent buff hôtel on the rue des Saints-Péres. Apparently the entire building had been raised and reinforced by the architect to accommodate a bomb shelter painted in white and equipped with beach furniture. I was much impressed though it was outdone by that of the Chase Bank, of unparalleled magnificence with a bar and bridge tables.

Lady Decies' son told me as we devolved along the chilly length of an unused ballroom on our pilgrimage to dinner that all his brandy bottles had been cracked by rattling against one another at bomb concussions. I fail to remember the spot, but considered the data interesting. One did not discuss the war at such dinners and it was quite in order for the Egyptian Ambassador to tell the following escapist triviality, typical of what went everywhere for conversation which I set down in my Journal:

"It appears that he presented his young King with a two-faced clock, a Janus clock, with the injunction that it must be placed on the desk of the room in which it was H. M.'s custom to give audience that visitors might not unknowingly overstay their welcome.

"Farouk, who I am told at Charvet's has his dressing robes made a dozen at a time, replied with rare delicacy, for he said that

Charvet windows also prepared for war

when the Ambassador should call, he would hide the clock, and on just such an occasion, he did, a year later.

"'He never forgets,' concluded the diplomat, smiling with his head to one side, absorbed in the paternalistic pride he felt in the grace of his young monarch, and not a little in the honor the incident did him."

The Ambassador continued to speak of an accident he had had the same morning and I find:

"The streets are quite full of cars bearing the yellow license plates of the *Corps Diplomatique* much to the annoyance of cab drivers who are impotent to sue or swear in the event of crushed fenders and traffic tie-ups in the darkness. In war time the cloak of diplomatic immunity must be the most pleasant of robes."

Lady Decies was a quite skillful water colorist and she took pleasure in displaying replicas of the various coronets she had painted herself. Her interest in heraldry, achievements and robes was great as was the knowledge on these subjects she was always willing to share since her coronation robes were displayed in the windows of the Trois Quartiers, and later a painting of herself in these same robes was to have figured in the Salon.

For various reasons, I deemed it unpropitious to broach the subject of Maltese ambulances and decided to write a letter about it the next day. I thought the robes of Malta depicted in a suitable painting would be an artistic counterpoint to the scarlet robes of a peeress and so noted in my letter in suitably delicate terms.

I soon received an answer which included a listing of Lady Decies' many honors and advanced a statement to the effect Lady Decies would not consider receiving a decoration from any but a chief of state. I felt I had been crushed between the weight of the Princess and the Peeress and slightly the worse for my adventure extricated myself a wiser man.

Though I ruefully observed that the columns of the *Herald* did not again note my presence at the rue des Saints-Péres, I was to become associated in one way or another with four more ambulance corps before the year was out: with that of Monsieur Bernard Fäy and Comte Etienne de Beaumont; that of the American Hospital under Thérése de Caraman Chimay; the Polish American Ambulance Corps, of which I served as secretary; and Ambassador Biddle's stepson, Schulze's Polish American Volunteer Ambulance Section or PAVAS, in which I inadvertently served as a driver during the battle of France.

One day I was having lunch at the Crillon with Miss Henrietta Ely. She is friend to most French generals, and particularly Marshal Petain, who had urged her to continue the work which had won her the Legion of Honor and the Croix de Guerre with palms for valor in the field, as well as many other decorations and the *fouragères* of three regiments. In fact I have heard soldiers call her "Mon Général" instinctively. She was telling me of her canteen at Metz which she had had decorated for the officers of General de Condé by Vertés who was serving as a second-class private. Like few artists, he was put to use where his abilities might be best applied.

It was a standing joke among the French that men were obliged to do jobs for which they were not fitted. Most of these were puns and I remember one which is translatable. The allocating sergeant is receiving a conscript, and with a questionnaire before him and fine pen raised he asks:

"Profession?"

"Butcher."

"Then we will let you tend the sausage balloon barrage."

At best the laughter was muffled.

In many places in Paris these anglophile balloons, semi-deflated, were lashed to ballast near cylinders of gas, particularly in the Bois, the Tuileries and along the Champs Elysées. I never saw them in the air, and one in particular must have had a leak since it appeared more anemic each day I passed it on my way to work.

Little did I think as I chatted inconsequentialities at the Crillon with Miss Ely that I was to escape with her from France into Spain on June 25, 1940, crossing the frontier but a few hours before the Gestapo took over.

She presented me to Miss Hoity Wiborg who asked me to cocktails the next day at her apartment which was that on the Quai de Conti in which Philippe Egalité was arrested with his mistress before being executed.

The Grill at the Crillon was virtually a club as were the cafés of Paris before the first Great War; the clientèle was faithful and limited. Every day Elvire Popesco, for whom Bernstein had written his play *Elvire*, then showing at the Ambassadeures, might be seen seated with some fortunate gentleman lunching at her favorite table. I saw this play which concerned an Austrian refugee, Elvire, in Paris. The reality of her past suffering is compared to the triviality of the problems of one of her French friends, yet she has been raised to such a plane by her torment ("Ils m'ont tout ôté, même mes mémoires") that she is incapable of loving, a fact which is the despair of one of the men and of a chastening effect on the other women. I should think translated, the play might have a great vogue here since it is an elation and synthesis of every refugee story to date.

I attended the play with Adrian Goekoop whom I had known before the war. He was Attaché de Presse at the Dutch Legation and possessed a lovely apartment on the rue Raynouard overlooking what had been the exposition grounds with the Eiffel Tower rising so surprisingly from their midst. Often after curfew he would take the entire orchestra from the night club Schéhérazade home with him as well as the dancers and singers, cold chickens, magnums of champagne and any officer and his companions who wished to come whether he was known or not. I remember riding through Paris lying (with a British aviator) on the rack affixed to the roof of a taxi, the inside being full; as we watched the branches pass between us and the gray moonlit sky overhead, he discussed his fear and consciousness of death in the strange impersonality he must have felt in such unusual surroundings.

Our groups at times were very gay, the nucleus being Pierre and Mano de Douville-Maillefeu, neighbors of Normandy; the first was an interpreter with the B. E. F., the second a subaltern in the 18th Chasseurs à Cheval, a cavalry regiment which was the first to enter German Territory where it remained fifty days. His father had been in the 17th Chasseurs during the last war, a regiment which had been abolished. Mano did his best to follow the paternal example in joining the 18th.

He told me that for the first three days of the war the French and German soldiers, though within twenty yards or so of one another, did not shoot. The French had orders to hold their fire until the seventh of September; evidently there had still existed hopes for peace. Later Mano showed me his trophies which included Nazi flags and clothing of excellent material. "Far better than ours," he affirmed. His regiment was cited for the *fouragère* of the Legion of Honor and the regimental standards were so decorated for which Mano was justly proud.

Despite being a Chasseur—the Chasseurs are usually small men, the big ones going to the dragoon or cuirassiers regiments—Mano was over six feet three. An excellent horseman he was a sight to inspire terror as he charged, spinning his saber above his head, his horse stretched at the full gallop. He often practiced this movement of his wrist by seizing a bottle by the neck and twirling it in a circle, the exercise he concluded in cutting off the top just under the lip with a cut of his cavalry saber without knocking the bottle over. He informed me that sharpened saber blades, kept in drums of oil since the last war, were reissued to the cavalry in August in order to replace the dull ones of peace maneuvers.

There was always much absurdity at these impromptu parties of the rue Raynouard which in retrospect were lamentable yet not without interest as a clue to our lack of realization or perhaps of conscience (which is, in effect, but an appeal to give heed to the lessons of experience).

There is something magnificent in the fact of the night clubs of

London today, but little is to be admired in the festivities of Paris before May, 1940. And yet we might have smelled the smoke of our Vesuvius.

Adrian and I were usually the only civilians. Others were a mysterious guards officer with a pseudonym whom the ladies whispered was a Scottish peer of the Intelligence Service traveling to Constantinople (he lagged long enough in Paris!) on affairs of direst import; or A. de Polignac with whom I made a bet. I had seen him at a ball two years before playing the drums in an impromptu solo much in the manner of any young extrovert. Now he replied that he would not be living to collect winnings from me since he was an aviator. This uttered in loud tones to the smiling adulation of the ladies present. He did not know what he said, yet today I should respect him. Then it went against one's nature to take the military seriously since that they did very expertly themselves, and very little else, and all to their eminent satisfaction.

As I write I cannot but remember our lightheadedness. There was an assumption of seriousness which was not in the least felt. We were unconsciously waiting. We played while we might as if that which we did depended on the turn of future events was in effect quite useless. We were resigned and waiting, and from this distance, rather pathetic and certainly in bad taste.

The next day I was able to find a taxi to drive to the Quai de Conti and cocktails at Miss Wiborg's apartment. It had become bitterly cold. It was strange this cold for which we soon acquired an intimate loathing as for an animate thing and the suffering it brought gave it all of a malevolent personality.

I was driven in the Winter gloom to the wind swept square on the Seine. The mighty buttressings cast shadows reminiscent of Rembrandt on the gray-brown and massively rusticated walls to the flickering of the corner lanterns. The place is excellent setting for scenes of medieval affray, for alarums and the clash of blades and deeds of bloody violence.

Within, I found after ascending the red carpeting to the chink of brass rods, a high-ceilinged apartment painted by Bakst as a scene from his *Belle au Bois Dormant.* In the gloom, an Italian was seated between Sir Michael Duff, who was unhesitatingly presented as "of the British Intelligence," and Mrs. Ian Campbell whom I was informed in undertones was to be the Duchess of Argyle. She is a lovely woman and made me think of one of Sargent's "Three Graces," with coils of hair about her small head.

I asked if the house were haunted by Philippe Egalité or by any of those who had come to seek him in a tumbril. As in answer to my light question the French window blew open with a clatter upsetting a little table. As we felt the sudden cold and dismal swish of the wind, Mrs. Campbell uttered a little shriek and I believe we felt intimations of torment and tasted the bitter ashes of love left by our treacherous predecessor in the fenestrated salon.

Eventually we played games, two of which I remember as having played as a child, for on one of us leaving the room, the rest decided on a common acquaintance, and the person who had left the room was recalled, whereupon he was commanded to ask us of what species of animal, plant or mineral the individual chosen made us think. From our answers, it was hoped he might derive the individual's identity. The other game was to send someone out as before, but to choose some object and to concentrate on it while the person sent out, having returned, endeavored to apprehend what was chosen from the violence of our concentration.

Surprisingly enough this last worked astonishingly well, and I assume the atmosphere sympathetic to psychical experiment.

An hour later, I left with the Italian gentleman. Above the motor coughing on its wretched gas, the howling of the wind, the rushing of the Seine and my own thoughts occupied with the cold I felt, I heard the muffled thunder of the D. C. A. greeting some aerial prowler of the night.

I noted in my Journal:

"Yesterday, an announcement appeared in the *Journal Officiel* summarizing the new Decree Laws. There is much about the quantity of bean flour in bread and other technicalities for manufacturers and wholesalers. Those laws which affect the individual directly are that pastry shops and confectionaries are closed on Tuesday, Wednesday, and Friday, that one may still buy *croissants* and *biscottes*, but that restaurants are forbidden to serve more than 150 grams of bread per head if the price of the meal is more than 15 francs, or more than 300 grams if the meal is an even 15 francs or less. No more than two courses, including only one meat dish, may be served. In addition a soup or hors d'Oeuvres (limited to four varieties), a piece of cheese or dessert are authorized. Butter served separately is prohibited, except with dishes where it constitutes a special seasoning. And bars are to be shut three days in the week!"

Despite price regulations, the cost of living was rising with the subtlety of the tide.

The current joke was that one might have *baba au rhum* on Sunday only, since only on that day was one permitted to have both liqueur and pastry, the necessary ingredients of the delicacy.

And despite regulations, one might eat in June, 1940, in Paris such dishes as might be found nowhere else in the world.

In my perusal of the *Herald Tribune*, I noted that Admiral and Mrs. Long had returned from the Abbaye to their apartment in the rue de Lubeck. I went immediately to present my respects and to ask them of how they fared at Longues.

It was natural that the Admiral and Mrs. Long should return to Paris for there had been no bombings (in fact Major Guichard had advised me not to bother to go down to the *abri* during the alerts), and it had become bitterly cold at Longues.

Most of our neighbors had returned to Paris and the few remaining in Normandy were too cold to stir out and thought it unwise to use their small gasoline supply in visiting, for if one had no special dispensation such as Red Cross work, one was allowed but forty liters a month, about ten gallons. The problem of getting additional fuel was solved in many ways—if one had coupons left over at the end of the month one gave them to one's favorite *garagiste* who was thus enable[d] to sell the amount specified on that particular *bon* to an unfortunate motorist who had run out; perhaps the courtesy would be returned another time. Prior to the beginning of the war, my father had put in a small reserve of 400 liters to run our agricultural machinery consisting of a gasoline lawn mower and water pump. Occasionally I would draw on this supply for my own wants. Small cars such as the four horse-power Simca and seven horse-power Fiat and Peugeot were at a premium.

These cars, unbelievably small, essentially practical for civilian use, were for some mysterious reason taken up by the Army. Once I saw a column of a hundred or more painted in military drab proceeding along a highway at their maximum speed of 35 miles per hour. The bearded and helmeted drivers appeared strangely uncomfortable and certainly out of place at the wheel. To what use the little cars were put I can't imagine.

The refugee children had left Longues as well and the Admiral and Mrs. Long missed them. They had marched under the entry way and along the pebbled path to their meals three times a day. The piercing Channel fogs, which made the lichened walls sweat and abetted a green moss in sprouting over the surfaces and interstices of the flagstones of the courtyard, had driven the children away.

Mrs. Long, an ardent walker, had taken every accredited promenade of the region; to Port-en-Bessin where fish were bought for Prunier's at Paris, and one might eat unparalleled *langouste*; to Arromanches[2] where it had been our custom to bathe in Summer, changing in the knot-holed cabins standing all in a row in Madame Paris' bathing establishment specializing in seaweed treatment for rheumatics; to the ruins of feudal Argouges; to Maison, the chateau said to be among Voltaire's favorites, and now the property of Baronne Gérard whose daughter was the Duchesse

2. Arromanches was to become the British invasion beach known as "Mulberry Beach.

d'Harcourt and wife of our deputy; and, to Longues' amazement, to Bayeux and back—twelve kilometers or more. Indeed, had she needed it, Mrs. Long might well have found sufficient incentive for her pilgrimages in the villager's admiration of the ease with which she accomplished these arduous walks.

The Longs had two Alsatian maids in their service who were sent in to Bayeux occasionally with the baker of Longues in his unvintaged car to make the necessary purchases. But this arrangement met up with a snag for the baker kept his eye less on the road than on his fair passengers.

"So," Mrs. Long told me, "what with the cold of the countryside, the departure of the children, the vicissitudes of the marketing, and there being no apparent reason for our not returning to Paris, we have!" As for me, I was delighted.

The Admiral and Mrs. Long were excessively kind and would often let me stay to dinner which was most pleasant after the inevitable meals in restaurants. All Paris ate at the restaurants and for many reasons; either from febrility and the need to go somewhere and see someone, principally the continual flow of *permissionnaires* on brief holiday, or merely from the fact one had returned to Paris but tentatively and did not want to burden oneself with a cook. Yet I believe it was from a nervosity which was dispelled or at the least given a vent in the friendly interchanges of the bistros, cafés, restaurants and night clubs. All of Paris ate as well as ever, and most particularly in the night clubs of which there were a great profusion. I remember two in particular: that of Suzy Solidor where the walls were covered with paintings of her and her famous dog, and Lucienne Boyer's Chez L decorated in interlacing "L's" of delicate shades of blue about which fluttered doves of peace.

Mrs. Long told me our Major, in the administration of his power to requisition, had many clashes with Madame Guichard and our maid Jeanne, who had stayed on at the place with Philippe the gardener, her husband having been mobilized. The Mayor was a defeatist and in September had said he would rather that "all Poland be crushed than one hair of his son's head touched." Such a statement was quite naturally resented by Madame Guichard, for she had five of her own men in the war and in any case there had always existed a state of feud between them.

The Mayor, an antique dealer from Paris, put on airs and decorated his wretched property with bad sculpture and unsalable tapestries from his shop in an attempt to lend his home the appearance of a château. Once, having ordered wood, he told the forester to deliver it "to the château"; the wood was delivered at the Guichard's woodshed. The Mayor never got over it and was recurrently apoplectic in private.

In June, when Mandel took over the Ministry of the Interior, Mayor Lefortier with many others was arrested. He doubtlessly occupied a position of trust under the German régime.

One evening, the Admiral purchased two tickets for a show and feeling disinclined to go himself, thought of me. I noted in my Journal:

"Yesterday evening I spent at the *A. B. C. Revue.* Situated deep in Montmartre, it is a thoroughly French institution much appreciated by bearded *permissionnaires* who I am told consistently jam the boxes, seats and standing room, much enjoying impromptu sallies by the actors. A skit, *The Marriage of Doctor Faustus*, with an actor of attenuated masculinity representing Hitler in the title role, was greeted with wild laughter and roars of approval. Hitler sits brooding in a sorcerer's chamber surrounded by phials and retorts labeled 'graisse de Goring,' 'ersatz,' and less topically 'KK.' Mephistopheles is summoned and appears as Stalin. Hitler is married to the latter's daughter, Bolsheva, who beats her husband over the head with a sickle and hammer to the accompaniment of stamping, applause and shrieks of delight from the audience. Next the Franco-British 'liaison' is celebrated in the one manner the French stage interprets the word, and the curtain comes down on an immense success, for the war is easily taken in the stride of Gallic humor, the blackouts giving rise to endless, funny situations.

"I battled my way to the doors and sprinted for a cab—of some 11,000 which functioned before the war, 8,000 are left, but their drivers have become unbearably snobbish and unpleasant, asking where one wishes to go. They are quite capable of not taking one if the address does not suit their convenience. Every dog has his day.

"I remember an unpleasant and quite typical experience. I had gone to the Avenue du Bois de Boulogne to call for an acquaintance. On arriving at the indicated address I asked the driver to wait, but he refused unless I pay him what I owed. I considered his request unusual and unwise since he might leave me stranded in that rather desolate region, and so refused, whereupon he leaped from his seat and threatened to bash in my head with a wrench. I looked for a policeman, but none was about and the fellow and I stood face to face in the dim light of a hooded lamp post, but not for long.

"I paid, and he departed with oaths and a petulant roar of his derelict motor.

"This evening at 8:30, on the Avenue President Wilson, I saw the eery criss-crossing of searchlights, and soon after the noise of the D. C. A. They sound much as giant skyrockets, and the explosion of the shells, blindingly bright, would further corroborate this impression.

"The same night or morning, for it was 4:30 A.M., I was awakened by the *alerte* sirens. It is impossible to describe their strange and soul-affecting lament, for theirs is a sound I have never heard before; their inhuman cry rises on slow waves of sound, perhaps similar to Oedipian chorus, for are they not the accompaniment and prophecy of Tragedy?

"Thus there is often an *alerte*, without cause and conversely a raid without *alerte*."

The next morning the following article appeared in the *New York Herald*:

"Wounding of six by D. C. A. shell brings warning; one man

loses leg in accident…the Military Governor of Paris…issued a new warning for Parisians to seek shelter as soon as anti-aircraft batteries open fire…"

The spot of the wounding was a block away from the street where Mrs. Long and I had earlier watched the firing.

I was told in Vienna by a barnacled newspaperman three years ago, that the febrility of a nation was evidenced by the amounts of sweets and chocolates consumed. The cafés and pâtisseries in Paris are jammed, and there were a great many teas.

It was at one of Mrs. Long's afternoons that it was suggested I pay my respects to Mrs. Goodfellow who, with her lovely daughter Kitty, had taken the Van Renselaer's little house and garden just off the Avenue Henri Martin.

Kitty had a job in the American Hospital and, undismayed, she had stuck to it despite the unpleasantness of the work at first and by way of test thrust on her.

Mano de Douville was on leave and with him I went to see Dallière, a friend of his of the same regiment who had been wounded severely in the arm, as well as Thérèse de Caraman-Chimay who was at the head of the American Hospital Ambulance Corps, and I thought at the same time I might present him to Kitty.

On arriving, we found Kitty had been placed in charge of Dallière since he was half American. Kitty, who arrived at the hospital every morning at 7:30 and did not leave till the same hour in the evening, said we must not stay too long and then ushered us in.

His face was against the raised back of his bed and almost of the same color as his sheet to which was pinned the yellow and green and gold of the Médaille Militaire and the Croix de Guerre with palm. His arm was immobilized at his side, and a cigarette hung from his lips beneath a trim military mustache. The superiority he had derived from suffering was evident in his eyes. Mano and I gave him the candy we had purchased for him and soon left. A wounded man was a rarity.

Once outside, Mano told me Dallière had been scouting on foot in no-man's-land with his brother-in-law when a plate-mine had exploded under their feet, almost wrenching off his arm and felling his brother-in-law by his side. The explosion attracted enemy fire, yet with his left arm he carried the body of his brother-in-law for some distance. Then realizing him to be dead; he stumbled back alone.

I noted in my Journal:

"Mano said he was troubled with frozen feet and spoke of patrol duty, of *corps à corps* fighting, of feud and ambush and night alarms reminiscent of our frontier encounters or more recently the guerrilla tactics of the Spanish Civil War. So individual in nature has become the night fighting on the strip of ground separating the two impregnable Lines that there exist countless opportunities for exploits of individual daring and valor. Patrols venture into the dark *Wald*, of no-man's-land armed with revolvers and burlap sacks. The latter are thrown over the heads of unsuspecting sentries who are kidnapped from their lines. The method is hardly one readily to be associated with modern warfare…

"These 'cutting-out' expeditions are made more dangerous by the presence of numbers of small or plate-mines. The wounds resulting from their explosions are usually in the legs; the large base hospital which I visited at Besançon was full of such cases. The anti-tank mines explode only at contact with objects heavier than a man. Mano affirmed that on suspect territory he had been given orders to go at a full gallop for thus he might escape the full effect of a mine blast, in the event of his horse setting one off.

"…At the front all communication and supply is done with horses. Six or eight are harnessed to small wagons. They go at a full gallop over the muddy roads. The advantages are manifold—no gas, no sticking in the deep ruts, and there exists a great demand for the beasts, as witness the presence of the French horse-purchasing commissions in New York, Chicago, Kansas City, St. Louis and elsewhere… Horror stories, true or untrue, have begun to circulate and the latest is that booby traps are made by the Nazis of dead soldiers left on the field.

"The often heard refrain, as familiar as the shrug of the shoulders by which it is usually accompanied, is not untrue, because this strange war is 'une drôle de guerre.'

"Opinions as to the duration of war vary from ten years to an equal number of weeks, but with Spring a majority believe the Germans must strike lest they lose their numerical superiority in the air—yet all is rumor, and the public are less gullible than in the early days of the war. They are much interested in and there exists considerable speculation concerning a third term for President Roosevelt; there is no doubt that the full strength of Allied propaganda in America is being kept in check until after the elections."

How archaic is the ancient history of my busy journal!

"...Frenchwomen have always been of heavier calibre than French men, but in Paris they prove themselves less frivolous than English women, deprecating feminine militarism and refusing to appear in uniforms save by necessity as in the Princesse de Caraman-Chimay's ambulance unit attached to the American Hospital. Yet uniformed, or uniformless, the women take war admirably in their stride and all worked far more than the men of the Maginot Line: e.g., on the rue St. Honoré at the corner of the rue de Castiglione, I saw two women unloading a truck. One placed vast packages on the back of the other who tottered to a doorway and there placed her loads on an elevator. Outraged, I sprang forward to assist, as had evidently several other men, for she waved me casually away as if from habit and said, 'Don't you bother, it's for Elizabeth Arden's.'

"Apparently the sturdy woman was carrying in packages of vials and unguents for the beauty establishment. I desisted from my attempt at interference assuming that in so doing I might interrupt a reducing scheme. It's the women's fault chivalry is dead."

My brother and sister had known Thérèse de Chimay years before. She asked me to write an article about her ambulance corps which I was most glad to do, and told me of how she held a man on his stretcher for an entire night as the ambulance felt its way to Paris from the East over the materiel crowded, blacked-out roads. Since he was mad with pain, despite numerous injections of sedatives, she was obliged to sit on his chest to keep him quiet. Such a contact with actual warfare was rare indeed, and those who later were to see people dying all about them turned their heads in the streets and stared their sympathy at the sight of the then rare wounded.

In an organized society as that of Paris in which each "circle" is geared with the next, one thing will lead to another. The Longs presented me to Kitty, and I should not have otherwise met Thérèse who would not have been able to tell me of Mr. Kemp's plan for the Polish American Ambulance Corps.

With the defeat of the Polish National Army in Poland, the auxiliary Polish Army in France became the Polish National Army and the division or more which it composed was recruited from Polish miners who had retained their citizenship though working the mines in the East of France, from Polish refugees and the small remnants of the Polish Army which had managed to escape from Nazi lightning; though largely supplied by the French it urgently needed equipment of every sort.

Mr. Kemp wanted someone to act as President of an American committee to be charged with raising funds to provide this new Polish National Army with ambulances. Mr. Dean Jay of Morgan and Company suggested my father who was intimately acquainted with Poland since he had served three years in Warsaw as financial adviser to the Polish Government. Father accepted on condition Mr. Kemp secure an official request for ambulances from the Polish President, Monsieur Raczkiewicz, which might be presented to the meeting of the Polish American Students' Association in

Chicago on January 1, 1940. By so doing he hoped to enlist their assistance at their annual conclave.

Ambassador Biddle joined Mr. Kemp, Mr. Singer and me, for I had been asked by Mr. Kemp to be Secretary of the Committee, and we went to the Polish Embassy at the old Hôtel de Sagan to lay Mr. Kemp's plan and request before the Polish ministers.

Today it seems incredible, but Zaleski and Stronski, Minister of Foreign Affairs and Vice President of the Council, respectively, who stated the Army wanted military ambulances, were advised by Mr. Biddle and Mr. Kemp to specify that such ambulances as should be purchased would be used for both civilian and military purposes, since a request for purely military ambulances might be looked at askance in America as a breach of neutrality.

Professor Vice Premier Stronski then agreed to send the necessary telegram to my father in the name of Monsieur Raczkiewicz and we all paraded solemnly out.

The Hôtel de Sagan appeared so magnificent in comparison with the heroic but shattered Polish Republic, with the tattered Polish flag depicted on a red-cross poster in the anteroom, that I was more strongly afflicted than before with an appreciation of the horror in loss of country. I thought of this tragic embassy, and of others like it in every capital of the world representing all that was left of Poland. And then I thought as well of the equivocal history of this hôtel, of the Prince de Sagan bribed by his estranged wife, Anna Gould, to stand at her side as she received Edward VII; of Boni de Castellane's remark on being questioned as to whether one of the lackeys clad in scarlet were a cardinal, "Oh, no, it is a *bon-homme* I placed near the stairway to give it a dash of color," and of Proust's dread when he first came to lay his homage and the eternity it implied, at the feet of "Madame la Duchesse de Guermantes."

From America we heard not a word for a month; then a letter from Father asking why the request was not sent.

Three weeks later Stronski confessed to Mr. Kemp, Morty Singer and myself, with tears in his eyes, "Que l'on ne peut pas tout faire soi-même"—that one must do everything one's self, that the telegram had not been sent. Such inefficiency was, in effect, an example of the results of that fratricidal political warfare the Poles waged amongst themselves. They could not forget their inner dissensions, remember they were of the same blood, and face the common enemy. Later, we learned the cabinet had been reshuffled with Professor Stronski the loser and the telegram had been forgotten in the mêlée. As a result my father could not address the Polish-American students on the subject of ambulances since he had no official request for such vehicles from the Polish Government to transmit. Unfortunately, the students met but once a year and it was to be several months before another group of Polish origin was to be organized large enough to assume the burden of collecting funds for such a unit in the face of the then prevalent anti-war sentiments in America.

Yet another example of the wastage inherent in political maneuverings was Monsieur Mateshewski, he who had so subtly smuggled the national gold reserve from Poland.

On hearing that he was in Paris with his wife, I hastened to present my respects to Madame Mateshewska. I found them in a little apartment on the Avenue President Wilson and was given coffee and cakes in accordance with the Polish custom at five in the afternoon. It is of Oriental origin, this coffee drinking on meeting and a surprise is felt if it is refused.

Madame Mateshewska, a head taller than her husband, in being her husband's antithesis was admirably his complement. Of a truly Grecian beauty, she had been the woman's, and for that matter I am tempted to say on my own authority, the *hors-concours* champion discus thrower of Poland. M. Mateshewski, a Governor of the Bank of Poland, explained to me that the gold was gotten out by the subterfuge of a heavily guarded column of twelve empty trucks following a direct road with the German aviation and tanks in hot pursuit, while a virtually unguarded column bearing the bullion proceeded by a more circuitous and apparently unsuspected route to the frontier.

The intensely quick eyes of the financier flicked behind his thick spectacles as he told his story with less accent and emotion than that expressed by his wife in her pleasing banalities. It was sad that such a man and soldier—for he was a colonel in the reserves—who had done much for his country along patently nonpartisan lines should not have been made use of and given the position of trust he so obviously deserved and might have occupied to the common good. In the words of a Polish gentleman of my acquaintance, the Slav is incapable of crediting the Anglo-Saxonism of the Loyal Opposition, for compromise is not an expedient but a subterfuge in Central Europe. Another remarked when I lauded Monsieur Mateshewski, "Oh, but he was paid!"

Later I was to have the pleasure of lunching with Mateshewski, Morty Singer, Cabestan (my friend of the Quai d'Orsai) and Krakowski, the son of the Polish philosopher, at Pierre's in the rue Daunou. Morty was just back from the Maginot Line which he had visited with General Huntziger. He said within it had the appearance and gray paint of a battleship. It is strange how people will repeat with a new conviction that which they have recently themselves witnessed though they knew of it before by hearsay.

Krakowski had lived in France for the greater part of his life and had served as the liaison between the French Chamber and the Polish Embassy. He knew and was known by most deputies and senators and understood the eruptive and mutating ideologies and idiosyncrasies of French officialdom. Besides, he had found time to write books on divergent topics.

Monsieur Krakowski I had met at the Salon of Madame Barthélemy, and he proposed to Jean Cabestan, with a typical respect for the circuitous, that I write an article for the *Tribune des Peuples*, a magazine to be modeled on the famous *Revue des Deux Mondes* which he, Count Mohle and Monsieur Lechon, counselors of the

Polish Embassy, had decided to publish with a "view to spreading Polish Culture."

Later we met in Cabestan's apartment to discuss the topic of the article and principally to hear Krakowski who was a fount of information on all subjects. Cabestan as well was an astonishing fellow. He had every known degree, in France the criterion of what one may do in life, and had been attaché at Berlin and Moscow. At thirty he spoke English, German, Yiddish, Russian, Croat, Jugoslav, Polish and Italian, this last sufficiently well to chat with Pozzo di Bergo.

In May, 1940, he became assistant to Foulques du Parc, the head of the radio censorship, and received folders with his name ingratiatingly printed thereon from *Havas*, the news agency, containing the releases to be censored. A teletype stood in the corner of his room and on June 1st, at the Quai d'Orsai, he showed me a bulletin which had just come in. Two German motorcyclists had arrived at the gates of Paris there to be disarmed at the Octroi! "It is the end!" he said. "Just like the Uhlans in the last war. Only now there's no Gaileni and what good could *he* do? What good are taxis against a Panzer division? One can't send a taxi against a tank today." And he put his thin ascetic face to one side, hunched his shoulders and walked to the window.

Outside the green dossiers containing reports and diplomatic correspondence were being piled into waiting trucks. They might as well have been left since they could be of no use to the Germans and had been of little to the French. "They're sending most of the Bureau to Tours," he said, without looking at me. We had made plans, Cabestan, Goekoop and I, to follow the Government in Goekoop's car, with a trailer behind carrying a tent and complete camping equipment with interchangeable flags—American, Dutch, and French—but our plans never materialized and Jean Cabestan who is on the peace commission at Wiesbaden left Paris, his library and his strange accumulations from travels in the Near East, to pedal South on a bicycle a day before Paris fell. Of Goekoop I have no word, and I spent June with the Polish Army.

After the discovery of the fiasco of the telegram-which-was-not-sent, and interviews with General Haller at the Polish Government bureaus in the converted rooms of the Hôtel Regina (on the rue de Rivoli opposite the Louvre) it was agreed to telephone my father from the Embassy to see what other group might be interested in taking charge of the collection of funds under my father's guidance.

General Haller, once called "the Pétain of Poland," was a sad figure in comparison to the magnificent drawing of his once boar-like head hung behind him as we visited him in his little makeshift corner room at the hotel. Yet it was evident from the fire of his eyes that his spirit was much the same as in the days of glory when he had led his Polish lancers against the Bolsheviki on the Eastern Front. He gave us a much beringed hand, and though obviously a sick man, expressed his determination to fly to America to collect funds. Contrary to the belief of inner circles at Paris, he was successful on his mission. One Polish gentleman to whom General Haller was unsympathetic said disparagingly on the General's return, "Pooh! He has collected only nine million dollars." I said nothing.

On the telephone at the Embassy from which we called to evade the meters of red tape ordinarily enshrouding such a step, I heard my father's calm and familiar voice stating that he believed the Polish Association of Doctors and Dentists under the able Presidency of Dr. Czwalinski of Chicago—the largest "Polish city" in the world after Warsaw since it included a population of 250,000 people of Polish extraction—might undertake the strenuous task of collecting the necessary funds from a disorganized and apathetic America.

I say disorganized, yet actually the fault at that time lay in too much organization, too great a diffusion of energies in the work of relief arising from chicanery and a lack of cooperation.

He asked for material for publicity; questionnaires from the Polish Government relative to the qualifications of volunteers, as well as stories relative to the urgency of their need, and the like.

To give the organization standing in France, Mr. Kemp arranged with Mr. Hills, editor in chief of the Paris Edition of the *New York Herald Tribune*, to publish an article about our work, and it was suggested he write an editorial on Polish-American amity. I volunteered the names of Kosciuszko and Pulaski as a nucleus and the next day submitted to Mr. Hills the following article which was subsequently published:

U.S. MOBILE HOSPITAL UNITS DUE IN MAY TO SERVE POLISH ARMY

VOLUNTEER COMMITTEES HEADED BY CHARLES S. DEWEY AND ARTHUR KEMP HAVE RAISED FUNDS AND ORGANIZED MOST MODERN AMBULANCE AND OTHER OUTFITS

Mobile hospital units, the first of their kind to be used in Europe, are to arrive from the United States during May to serve the Polish National Army in France. Composed of mobile X-ray, dental, hospital, first-aid station and sterilization units as designed for the United States Army, in addition to trucks and ambulances of a more conventional nature, they represent the last word in the development of field service.

Under the presidency of Hon. Charles S. Dewey, former Assistant Secretary of the United States Treasury and Financial Adviser to the Polish Government from 1927 to 1930, from which he retained the position of permanent member of the Council of the Bank of Poland, and Commander of the Legion of Honor, the American Association of Polish Doctors and Dentists, headed by Dr. Peter F. Czwalinski, have undertaken the raising of funds throughout the United States, establishing for their purpose sub-committees of their American Committee for the Polish Ambulance Fund in cities and towns in which there existed Polish-American populations. The result has been an influx of funds from every state in the union.

It was Arthur T. Kemp who first organized the Committee for the Polish Ambulance Fund. President of the American Hospital at Neuilly from 1933 to 1938, among the first volunteers with the French Army in 1914, he served with two ambulance corps during the World War—the American Volunteer Motor Ambulance Corps, under auspices of the St. John's Ambulance and the British Red Cross, as well as the Norton Harjes Corps later attached to the American Red Cross. During the Spanish Civil War he served on the De Flores Fund Committee, sending some thirty-six field ambulances to the Franco forces.

Mr. Kemp has been awarded the Mons Star with bar by the British as well as the British Service Medal. He was made Officer of the Legion of Honor by General Joffre and received the Croix de Guerre with star. Later, he was decorated by the Spanish Government and given a captaincy in the Spanish Red Cross.

He considered in what manner he might best apply experience gained in the World War and the Spanish Civil War to the present conflict and decided personally to assist the Polish refugees in France. To this end he formed a committee numbering experienced friends and associates in earlier war services, Comte Charles de Chambrun, Mortimer Singer, Carlos de Florez, the Marquis de Mun, Harold Kingsland, and A. Peter Dewey. Mr. Kemp then offered his committee for the development of his plans to the newly formed Polish Government under President Raczkiewicz.

With the arrival in France of General Sikorski on October 1, enrollment in the Polish contingent increased. Originally conceived as a Franco-Polish auxiliary to Polish forces in Poland, this body of men became the National Polish Army.

Soon it became apparent to Mr. Kemp and his committee as well as to the Polish General Staff, the Polish Cabinet and to General Denain, chief of the Franco-Polish Mission, that a problem of Polish relief existed in France but was, in effect, principally the care of the embryonic Polish Army forming on its soil. As a result, from purely civilian aid, Mr. Kemp and his committee decided to organize an ambulance corps to cooperate with the Polish Red Cross in the urgency of its many duties.

General Sikorski, Vice Premier Stronski, Minister of Foreign Affairs Zaleski, as well as General Haller and Ambassador Anthony J. Drexel Biddle, Jr., were consulted and their enthusiastic approval given.

Mr. Kemp envisaged the corps as possessing three committees; the working committee in France under Mr. Kemp, the other two in the United States, one for the purpose of raising funds under Charles S. Dewey, and the other an advisory committee composed of prominent Poles of which Princess Radziwill, now in Paris, is a member.

With the equipment will come Polish-American doctors, dentists and experts to work with Mr. Kemp's foreign committee and the Polish National Red Cross.

The American committees are successful in their work throughout the United States and will have continuing value not only during, but after the present war.

I had done my best to make the article appear impressive.

The last of these committees was an invention of mine to secure the support without interference of various nice ladies—they might help to collect funds but not interfere with Mr. Kemp in the actual running of the ambulances and have no say as to policy.

We felt we had done everything that we could until we received word from America and so we waited.

Mr. Mowrer had departed for the United States planning to spend the Christmas holidays with his wife and daughter, but the Clipper was grounded for two weeks at Horta, in the Azores—undoubtedly a severe trial on the patience of any individual and most particularly a journalist.

For the interim, his desk was occupied by another correspondent and I secured permission to leave Paris once again to buy my ticket for Besançon at the Gare de l'Est and resign myself to the mummification which was travel in France in the Zone Militaire.

During my week in the Haute-Saône I felt the bitterness of complete and utter cold. At night I did not undress but slept in my paneled chamber with its twenty-foot ceilings and the windows closed with all my clothes on and my feet against the zinc water bottle. The eiderdowns were piled in an immense heap above me, and I slept with the ancient linen sheets over my face. The threads were round and separated as in gauze.

In the vast hallway from the walls of which grinned the heads of boar and wolves with their tarnished brass notices underneath bearing the place and date of the kill, the temperature was but two degrees above freezing.

The dining room was passably warm though at meals we were forced to sit in our overcoats. The bats in their lodgings between the wainscoting and the wall died in great number and the stench from their decaying bodies was terrible. The chateau, a huge pile which had been built in the eighteenth century by the seigneur as an improvement over his feudal castle, a farm in the valley below, had been used hitherto only in the summer, and the heating arrangements were sketchy.

After three months of training, my little cousin was an anesthetist in the operating rooms of the hospital at Besançon where lay in serried white cots three thousand wounded from foray and ambush in no-man's-land war. Though she was but eighteen and had been educated in the restrained fashion of little French girls, studying at a convent in the rue de Lubeck, she was most efficient at her work.

A month before, her parents being away, she had occupied their room above the kitchens since it was warmer. At midnight, she was awakened by a stone flung against her window, and leaning out in the strange, blurred night of moonlight and snow, she saw the farmer's son.

"Mademoiselle, come quickly, the Serb is having her baby."

On with her shoes and coat. She descended the echoing stairway in the darkness under the boar and wolves, turned the massive key in its lock and let herself out into the brown night and descended the hill past patches of snow glowing in the night. The wind blew without haste and she breathed through her mittens to protect her naked lungs and thought of what she would do.

The Serbs were an unmarried couple of refugees who had been imposed upon the château by the authorities as refugees from Alsace when Strasbourg had been evacuated—Strasbourg where all journalists wrote of hearing their footsteps echoing in the empty streets. The man did odd jobs about the farm, and the woman awaited her confinement like a cow.

My cousin found the Serb by the door smoking and sent him off for the doctor on his bicycle. He protested it was too far and she turned on him in wrath and he left. By the light of two candles guttering at the bottom of glasses to keep them from being blown out, she delivered the woman of her baby and placed it in her own fur coat in a potato box for lack of anything better.

The woman bled most horribly and the baby was malformed and my cousin prayed that it would live till the doctor came, and christened it herself. At last the chugging of a motor, the creak of a hand brake and the slam of a door; the doctor came in grumbling, his hair on end, his collar button gleaming at the throat of his collarless shirt, his pince-nez askew; he rolled up his sleeves, banished my cousin and mumbled, "Se déranger pour une pourriture comme ça..."

An hour later the baby died to be buried the next day in my cousin's coat. She attended the funeral nearby and, on her way back, was violently ill when she found herself stepping on a placenta lying by the door of the farm in the mud.

At Christmas time there was a tree, and all the little children of the village came to see it and be given bonbons and presents such as dart pistols and horns to toot. In particular, I remember a little lame one, a veritable Cinderella, since I had seen her the Fall before seated beside her father's fire—the man was the mayor of the village—solemnly peeling potatoes.

Christmas day there were several parties much lacking in *entrain* as a result of the intense cold; gentlemen who had been officers in the past war, attempted not to look self-conscious in their too-tight and outmoded uniforms, some with their ribbons protected under cellophane.

The same evening, I received a telegram from Ambassador Biddle to the effect that he would put me up at his château near Angers when I should go to that new capital of Poland presumably to photograph and write articles on the Polish Army training camps situated nearby.

Sorrowfully I soon left my friends to the cold, the blood-stained whiteness and anesthetic torpor of the operating rooms, to a war whose horrors were more real than any in France until June.

At Paris, I anticipated the customary fol-de-rol of securing necessary papers to visit the secret training camps which, so far as I now know, I was the only journalist to have entered. I was received with great courtesy by a Polish Major of Intelligence in his bathroom. Perhaps a word of explanation would not be amiss. So crowded was the hotel, that many officers, needing waiting rooms, and rooms for their secretaries, relegated themselves to the bathrooms

(opposite) Photo of Peter in Polish Boy Scout uniform inscribed to his sister (Louise.)

pertaining to their bedrooms that they might work in comparative private, the bedroom serving as reception room.

The Major's work table straddled the bathtub, and visitors were invited to sit on a w. c., sanctimoniously covered with a cushion. I admired the Major for completely ignoring our surroundings and shook his hand warmly when with a jingling of spurs he bowed me out with the necessary papers in my hand—one envelope for Coëtguidan, the other for St. Gemmes. On leaving I cautioned an amazed Polish scout who maneuvered the elevator with dexterity to "be prepared" in Polish, gave him a two fingered Polish boy scout salute and issued out into the street. At the age of ten I had served as a Polish boy scout and believe I am the only non-Pole ever to have so done, or for that matter thought of it.

Arrived at my apartment, I wrote my parents much the following letter:

...I have deferred writing about the job as I hesitated to form an opinion, as I quite naturally considered that it might be wise to wait at least three months...but perhaps I should explain the arrangements at the office.

Mowrer (in his absence another) does the writing and for this is in daily communication with the American Ambassador and other officials who are anxious to give him the "news" since he controls so vast a public opinion.

Ghali was secretary to his uncle, the Egyptian Ambassador, and has lived in Paris for some fifteen years. It is he who goes and sees the *attachés de presse*, one for each embassy, who disseminate their official information as well as an equivalent official for the Quai d'Orsai.

Taylor does all communication work and acts as Mr. Mowrer's personal secretary, securing tickets, etc.

When I arrived in Paris, Mr. Mowrer knew nothing of my coming, I assume, and as a result he had nothing for me to do. As each newspaper has the right to send out but one man on an assignment (to the Line, on a destroyer, etc.) Ghali and I, of course, never go.

My work consists in reading the newspapers and underlining for Mowrer, and I have been given countless little tasks to "keep me busy."

This *rien faire* which echoes the atmosphere of Paris is accentuated by the fact that there is nothing happening and the correspondents find it difficult to get one article out each day. Actually, before the war, Mowrer and Taylor were here alone.

My greatest "asset," if it were possible to apply it, is my endless fund of personal and "unofficial" friends and informants; individuals like Pierre, etc., who ask me to do the unusual things—go on an Allied aviation inspection tour, attend the christening of four railway howitzers, visit friends in their various camps, to wit: no less than six acquaintances in their regiments of mounted cavalry, motorized cavalry, student officer barracks, Red Cross, interpreters, and infantry, respectively. The incidents they might recite *could* be made into not uninteresting articles; but when I approached Mr. Mowrer with information concerning them he mentioned that he could not (quite obviously) use such information in his political articles. Thus, I consider my principal duty one of observation and this I have done and feel I understand the journalistic method. Ghali plans to return to Chicago after the war to get the "ground-work" of journalism, I should be obliged to do so in any event, were I to undertake journalism as a profession.

The question of "cheapening" communication is bogus—it is done as cheaply as possible already.

I was told to chart the prices from all points by various methods of transmission to Paris. To do so is virtually impossible as there is much complication with fluctuation in rates of exchange, price, gold values, etc. I set to it, however, and saw a man by the name of Huot in charge of Press Wireless who deemed the task an impossibility. He told me, however, that there was a price commission in Switzerland which might conceivably have the telephone rates per month for various countries. Huot himself uses a slide rule to figure out daily price quotations and equivalents from Holland! (Correspondents at other points pay at their end.)

Since I know the secretary of the Foreign Minister in Switzerland, I thought I'd go down to Berne. After securing the exit visas from France, I was told not to get the Swiss visa since Mr. Mowrer planned to go to Geneva (each paper is allowed but one permission to enter Switzerland from France without an inquest by the Swiss). At the last moment, Mr. Mowrer did not go, so I might as well have done so, and I was admonished to solve the problem by writing to the correspondents. I received no answers.

In the meanwhile, I have been writing on my novel and plan to send the opus in for the *Atlantic* prize competition but consider it will bear considerable improvement and is a bit brief (70,000 words only).

In short, I have acquainted myself with the methods of correspondents.

This is a very poor explanation of events pertaining to my work and there exist so many attenuating circumstances that on reading this letter over, I find it effectual at telling you that I have not done much in the way of journalism myself, yet it does not fully describe the benefits which I have received from observation not only of journalism, but of those methods of gaining ends, of "human nature" and of much indefinable experience, such as sitting in the waiting rooms of Ministers and corrupting minor officials!

I've rather had all the fat sweated off my methods of thinking and opinions and find men vastly different than I had thought them to be with you both near, and I have gained I believe a much more correct and solid opinion of my own capabilities, and my wants.

I have seen many types and thanks to you and others, move in different circles, but realize that I must now establish my own identity.

No, my time is not wasted and the book which you are surely bored with hearing about is good, *I* believe.

I find Paris business operated with a pleasantness as if the machinery had lost many of its rough edges. Is it because the old and wise and experienced are again at the various tillers having been recalled from their philosophic dotage and inactivity of peace?...

My life in Paris is very full, while in the country I live the contemplative life, writing of what I've done—I find it most pleasant...

The same evening Kitty had her birthday party and we, her guests, a most outrageous but highly enjoyable time at Monseigneur. Impersonating a Hungarian, I told the manager that should he decrease the bill I would bring more "American sheep for the shearing." Everyone was delighted when he confided he would knock off twenty per cent. I felt pleased for Kitty at the time, but rather sad the next morning. These night clubs like Monseigneur, and fire-gutted Casanova, and Schéhérazade with their authentic and sybaritic gilt and guilt and candle-light were rapidly becoming extinct.

I remember the service which made them perfect. One September I went to Casanova, and faced with the imposing scroll bearing the vintages and prices of various champagnes I ordered the one most adaptable to my purse. A year later I returned with a lady it was my hope to impress with my worldliness. I gave my last franc to the headwaiter when he intoned, "The customary bottle, Sir?"

At one A.M., I mounted my red-rugged stairway, my hand touching the curved wall in the dim blue light, and humming a tune—it may well have been the German favorite, *Oh, we'll hang out our washing on the Siegfried Line*—I sought for my key, when suddenly on my landing I became transfixed. My door was open. Inside, all my drawers lay on the floor and the bed clothes were torn off and flung to the ground. I stepped back onto the landing where there was a chest of drawers heaped with sand bags to extinguish incendiaries, opened the bottom drawer and found my briefcase containing my letters of introduction and various papers. I considered reporting the matter to the police, but thought it useless. My opinion was confirmed by Jean Cabestan, whom I notified in a guarded conversation of what had happened—a friend who spoke English had warned me that with two hundred others he worked in shifts to censor English telephone conversations in Paris alone.

Jean came over and sat by the fire and with a glass in his hand observed me as I put things to rights and asked, looking at me narrowly, what I might possess. I answered, "Nothing," then thinking of my permission to go to the camps I added "except this," handing the buff envelope to him. It was inscribed in Polish. He read it, then handed it back with a laugh saying "Don't be an ass, twenty per cent of the soldiers in those camps are spies." Discomfited, I wondered what had been sought—perhaps *they* didn't know either. In any event my concierge, who seemed to change every day—the job was unpopular as the result of the intermittent yet continuous jangling of the night bell—knew nothing whatsoever; I soon forgot the matter in hastening to the Angers train at the Gare d'Austerlitz the next afternoon.

On every side, as I unfolded my paper in the carriage, I heard Polish spoken. The train clickety-clacked through the countryside, and when it became too dark to read by daylight, the curtains were drawn and the light put on in defiance of the printed notice. No one seemed to care, least of all the ticket collector who bowed and saluted a brigadier sitting opposite me. At the stop at Tours, the latter came to life and from my *Herald* lazily surmised me to be English and condescended to speak, perhaps to exercise his English: "They do not care about the light here, the Boches never come this far," and crossing his hands over his stomach he relapsed as if he had uttered a good joke.

In June, I was to remember his words while watching dog fights over Tours, and heartily cursed the generals.

At Angers, which was unusually God-forsaken, I found the suave Mr. Elbrick who was Chargé d'Affaires, since Ambassador Biddle had quit Angers to take Mrs. Biddle from their moated and medieval chateau for a stay at the Meurice that she might recuperate from a touch of cold. In addition, he was First Secretary, Second Secretary, Naval, Air, Military and Commercial Attachés all efficiently rolled into one.

Most courteous, I had first had the pleasure of meeting him in Warsaw two years before. His escape from Poland he was to narrate later in the evening, for since I had no place at which to stay, he kindly offered to put me up at the château he and his witty wife had taken in the environs. To pass the time until my host was prepared to leave for his home I wandered about the town with which I had but little acquaintance. It was virtually black since the Poles were continually threatened with extermination from the air by the Traitor of Stuttgart, the French equivalent of Lord Haw-Haw, since it was no secret to the Germans that Angers was "Poland."

Though the shops did a booming business—the Polish troops were well paid due to Mateshewski's work in getting out the gold, and had little stickers in their windows stamped with a Polish eagle surrounded with the legend "Vive Poland, Brave and Faithful!"—the inhabitants were a bit uneasy at the doubling of their population and the liability it implied. A liability of which they were constantly reminded by Stuttgart.

At a pastry shop, I had some chocolate and Polish cakes and observed the well turned-out, black-booted officers. Though the majority were fine soldiers, a small minority who had purchased their commissions were not well regarded by their men with whom they were arrogant, and much bad blood existed between the Poles and the French. The French could not help but sneer at the rapidity with which Poland had fallen and their thought, "It is for such people that we are at war," was often half spoken. During the Battle of France, when the first Polish Division refused to retreat to internment in Switzerland but stuck to their posts fighting tanks with the magnificent courage of Warsaw and wine bottles filled with gasoline to be annihilated to a man, their battle cry, "We do this in return for the hospitality of France!" I feel was ironic.

Even in the highest quarters of the Franco-Polish Mission I have heard the Poles and their methods spoken of with scorn and their integrity slightingly shrugged at. There is no doubt the French who associated with the Poles felt they supported an unworthy cause.

The Poles, among the proudest and most warlike people living, yet sensitive, felt these intimations of opprobrium; as things turned out their courage was as little to be criticized as anyone's. Yet the lack of cooperation in their own government, leading no matter what the motive to the results of untrustworthiness, was exasperating to all who had business with them.

Despite the calamity which had befallen Poland they were unable to forget personal rancor. It is the one fault of this fine people and yet it is to their eternal disgrace. There is no doubt that the

French suffered from a similar disease. It has by now become a platitude that Nazism thrives in the interstices of the bricks forming political entities, bricks which must be firmly cohesive for a national solidarity.

I shall remember the scorn of a French officer of my acquaintance as he spoke of seeing Polish officers gorging at a restaurant. I restrained myself from answering that the French were the last people on earth to criticize others for paying too much attention to the stomach. Perhaps the Poles and French committed identical patriotic sins in different ways.

I returned to the Embassy offices at seven and drove with Mr. Elbrick to his château in his American car which still bore Rumanian license plates. In passing through the various villages, my host pointed out a Czech general mobilization poster shining wanly in the ghostly-blue light of an intersection lantern.

With the Ambassador, Mr. Elbrick had endured much of the siege of Warsaw before leaving the capital with the Polish Government. Mr. Biddle later told me that a Stuka had left a pit "big enough for ten horses to be buried in" at the center of the cobbled court of the Rascynski Palace leased by the Ambassador in the heart of Warsaw. Later the lovely hotel was entirely destroyed. I well remember its cartouches of crimson damask, its Savonnerie and Aubusson, which inspired the French to erect their vast, ugly, modern Embassy, now gutted, to preserve their prestige. The splendor of the American Ambassadresses' receptions, particularly that for which thousands of roses were flown from Holland, was the wonder of Central Europe. But all such pleasantness is past, the days of balls and visiting potentates, perhaps the most amusing of which was that which marked the arrival of the King of Afghanistan.

His Royal Highness had visited Paris and there, in accordance with royal prerogative, he had paid calls at establishments of every sort, charging jewels and couture of inestimable worth and leaving the French Government ruefully to pay the bill. With horror, the

Minister of Finance at Warsaw heard the King intended to honor Poland with his presence, and the better shopkeepers gloatingly redid their window decorations and changed their price tags, in preparation for the day, after leaving their cards with the concierge at the Europejski Hotel, undoubtedly to the latter's satisfaction. Distraught, the Minister told his quandary to my father and was unsmilingly advised to declare an enforced national holiday for the duration of the King's visit.

The Afghan Potentate arrived to find a guard of honor, red carpeting at the station and maneuvers to review, but every shop window grated, every store shut. In the Stare Miasto or Old City, Fouguer's was barricaded, Fouguer's where stood the incomparable bottles of 1700 Tokay, tramped from grapes of the fifth row with stalagmites of ambrosia hanging from the loose corks; and the hoary tuns of centenarian Mead a few drops of which ruby opium leave a man's head clear but his feet heavy as lead.

The King stayed but one day, yet had his revenge, for that night at a ball, he espied a Cabinet Minister who had received a decoration of the rank of commander from the Afghan Government. The Polish gentleman was renowned for his collection of emeralds; in fact, several had been set into the decoration resplendent beneath his white cravat. There is no doubt the oriental eyes of the Potentate caught the deep Caspian glint of the stones as the Minister bowed before him.

"Ah, but my dear Minister, such a decoration is unworthy of you, you shall have mine," and the King stripped the Minister of his emerald-studded cravat and invested him with his own grand cordon, an enameled cross and ribbon which might be bought in most good pawnshops in Paris for a few francs, "Hardly a fair exchange, you know," intoned the British Ambassador.

From Warsaw which had been so pleasant and was left a shambles of smoking rubble, torn bodies and narrow graves, Mr. Biddle and Mr. Elbrick retreated South stopping when did the Polish Government, and more often than not harassed on the road.

Le Rire, a French humorous magazine, reported that during the retreat a bomb fell just outside Mr. Biddle's window while he was shaving. In defiance, it was said, he hurled his shaving brush at the departing Boche. I have not authenticated the tale.

At the Elbrick château I was more comfortable than I had been for several months, since their well deserved diplomatic immunities allowed them quantities of coal. I enjoyed myself immensely and the joints of my fingers were not stiff from the cold for hours on end. In my apartment the only places I might be warm were my bed and the bathtub, and the latter but three times a week, Monday, Tuesday and Wednesday (the hot-water-days were not separated in order to avoid the wastage inherent in starting a new fire every other day). The rest of the time one remained dirty, but as an elegant but shivering lady told me, "La crasse, ça tient chaud." And of some people it was said with a disdainful curl of the lip, "He married for warmth."

The next morning, I reported early at the Polish Ministry, the heart and brain of exiled Poland, a large building on the main street just opposite the American Embassy. I was later to regret this governmental juxtaposition when in June I wandered in the sun-drenched garden with Sézanne, my dog, asking myself if I were a coward. The radio kept blaring Angers would be destroyed like Warsaw, and we waited in the hot silence of the evacuated city for death, and our two lost drivers rejoined us, their uniforms soaked in blood.

At the Ministry I photographed Monsieur Zaleski, whom I had last seen ten years before, Monsieur Ciechanowski, the present Polish Ambassador at Washington, and other gentlemen. I was given a card by a much bored young attaché to the French police so that I could secure a pass through the outer cordon of French Gardes Mobiles encircling the training camps; as in better days the formalities inherent in passing from one country to the next, though "the next" be fictitious, were scrupulously maintained.

Mr. Elbrick was kind enough to have an Embassy car and chauffeur put at my disposal, and I drove to have a look at President Raczkiewicz's château, the official seat of government. Fourteen ambassadors and ministers were accredited to Poland, and they and the French Ambassador, an anomaly, lunched and supped every day in the one tolerable restaurant of the town, the Vert d'Eau, with all the Polish Ministers. On seeing so many statesmen volubly eating their lunch I contemplated the carnage a bomb might do, and let myself consider the essential tactical hypocrisy of the World War I in which it was tacitly understood that neither German nor Allied G.H.Q. should be bombed or submitted to attack.

I photographed Cabinet Ministers in their frogged hunting coats and envied their warmth as I pressed the release of my Leica with a blue finger.

At President Raczkiewicz's château, I'd rather hoped that something might be doing but it wasn't, so I continued on to St. Gemmes. I had a letter to the colonel of what I discovered to be a regiment of engineers. After some difficulty, I found a captain and he dispatched a solemn boy of eighteen or thereabouts in a too-large uniform to take me to the colonel. The boy spoke French without accent, and somewhat surprised, I asked him how long he had been in France. "All my life," he answered. Like many others he was a miner from the East of France who had not relinquished his Polish citizenship and had the choice of the Polish or French Army in which to enroll himself.

Together we squelched solemnly through the mud and fine drizzle, my guide saluting whenever an officer passed, I raising my hat. It was a rotten day for pictures. At last we arrived to where the great man stood and after proper salutations, he turned me over to a major who tramped all over with me explaining just what the men were about.

Soon a column four abreast about a hundred yards long, came swinging by a road nearby. Instinctively I ran after them to get their photograph and was dismayed to feel the Major's hand like a vise on my arm. He shouted an order, the column wheeled and

Polish soldiers in WWI uniforms with French WWI Lebel rifles, France, 1939

marched past me. I was able to get some splendid pictures. The Major smiled benignly on me and I grinned back.

"Do you want them again?" he questioned. It was magnificent.

They were a fine group of men for the most part. Big, healthy and cheerful, they worked in their "polygons" as engineers term their grounds, constructing pontoon bridges over imaginary rivers, digging trenches in zig-zags to avoid enfilading fire, setting up barbed wire and filling fascines with dirt. In the distance beyond my scope of vision in the enshrouding grayness, I heard the harsh rattle of machine-gun fire and shouts and laughter. We passed a group of men with arms crossed or akimbo being lectured by a veteran. The rain matted their hair to their pink foreheads, and ran over their faces. "He is teaching them how to set up booby traps," explained the Major with a wave of his hand. I thought of François, a friend who had told me the Germans had set explosives in French corpses. When the stretcher bearers came for their dead, they remained with them.

Polish soldiers digging trenches *(above)*; setting barbed wire *(below)*

Pontoon bridges constructed by Polish soldiers

We passed a guard house; the Major had the guard turned out. Composed of four men and a lieutenant, it aligned itself smartly between two white staffs bearing French and Polish flags. I photographed them to their evident pleasure. They were simple, and did not grumble and are among the best fighting men in Europe.

I was shown the sleeping quarters, the few men present clicking to attention as the Major entered, their hands at their sides, palms out, their invariably shaved heads with a tuft of forelock back, the chin in. The quarters were crowded but dry, and the men slept on hay till bunks should be manufactured.

In the mess hall some hundred men were chanting in the chorded soul-unison the Slav discovers in music.

A young French lieutenant with the look of Montmartre in his eyes, and a cigarette dangling from his lips and a harp insignia on his lapels, was intently listening and jotted down the slow and solemn chant as the men evoked it.

In the corner was a Christmas tree covered with paper dolls and makeshift baubles and rifles stacked before it. I felt very sad, and remembered the first Polish Christmas tree, a monster one, my mother had set up in the Stare Miasto fourteen years before. It was covered with stars cut from mirrors, and the fire department had set up lights at the corners of the square. As the wind played with the stars, light was reflected in a thousand lovely ways to the evident enjoyment and "ohs" and "ahs" of the crowds. Evidently the custom had persisted.

Nearby in a farmyard, rolling kitchens were chocked, and a company drawn up at attention there was being served. As a man's name would be called he stepped forward into the cloud of steam surrounding the boilers, and shortly reappeared, his canister filled with a thick meat and vegetable soup and a piece of bread in his hand. I was offered some and thought it thoroughly palatable, yet one hundred times inferior to what "our boys" would tolerate.

Quite pointedly, I was taken to the infirmary, a little whitewashed building equipped with ten pallets, two of which were occupied.

Polish soldiers with food canteens

On one lay a big peasant boy with a pale face covered with beads of sweat. He attempted to sit up, but the Major kindly pushed him back, and said to me in a matter of fact way, "Appendicite." As always, normal sickness and disease seemed incongruous in a soldier. It was evident to what degree hospital units would be useful.

And yet again I think of the spirit of these men as they trained with such a will, attempting to do in six months what the French were taught in two years, and the Germans all their lives. And I think of the manner they went at it, so pleasantly, like boy scouts, or children on a picnic, and they were to be used against the Panzer divisions and annihilation.

I thanked the Major and once back at the car, offered him a bottle of brandy for the use of his mess. He shook his head, explaining that his officers had vowed not to drink till Poland had been reborn. I answered with all the sincerity I felt that I had been convinced Poland need not be reborn since it was quite evident she had never died.

Once back in Paris I arranged with Mr. Huot to have a dispatch sent to my father over the wireless the French authorities had put at the disposal of the Press combine. Strictly speaking, it was illegal to use this route for any messages save those of the newspaper stockholders of Press Wireless, yet we decided at Prunier's over a *pilaf de langoustine à l'Armoricaine* that if l paid the far cheaper rate than that which should be asked did I send my cable through the ordinary channels, the Government would most certainly not mind since the cause for which the message was sent was to the governmental benefit. And most certainly the stockholders would not object since the message was for charity's sweet sake. Moreover the sending would be at an hour which would not in any way interfere with their own schedules.

Through an employee, the journalist who had replaced Mr. Mowrer discovered our plan. I had not attempted to hide it from him but had merely not told him, considering it not his affair. Angrily he called me up at Press Wireless asking me by what right I sent dispatches without his permission, and though I explained as succinctly as possible, I'm afraid bad blood remained, and I saw little of him thereafter.

The innocent cause follows, and was translated and used in the Polish language press in the United States. Evidently, the *Chicago Daily* News never realized I had paid for the message since my father was dunned for it later.

> PARIS, Jan. 11.—The rafters of a barn in a province of France echoed the deep choir of a hundred voices. The patriots forming the exiled Polish Army were singing their martyred country's songs, yet in their voices was the courage of an undying optimism, of a hope which was conviction in representing the will to live itself. The eyes of the singers were dimmed with the memory of distant perspectives; and the nostalgia to look on that which inspired their song.

"Somewhere in France," the men stood in file to sing before a French musician that he might set their song on paper, for all Polish military sheet music had been destroyed with Poland, and yet the spirit of both the country and the songs are undying in these men....What the men do is easily described, how they rise at six, sing and exercise before breakfast, work during the morning, eat and work again, how they sit in the little village café and dream of Poland reborn from her still smoking ashes; yet how tell of their magnificent spirit, the bond of strong purpose which links officers and men, the will and desire to die if Poland may but live?

Without music or flags, these same troops marched before their chief, General Wladislas Sikorski, who as the world knows took command of the Polish Army, now forming in France, on October 1, 1939, simultaneously with his nomination as Premier by President Wladislas Raczkiewicz.

The troops passed their leader, their feet ringing on the frozen earth, their eyes met his, and a communion, a solemn accord was established in that fleeting instant. A question had been asked and answered. He would lead and they follow.

It is for these men who have lost everything save their patriotism that an ambulance is needed.

Władysław Raczkiewicz, President of Poland-in-exile *(on left)*, Władysław Sikorski, Premier and Commander in Chief of Polish Forces in exile *(on right)*, General Stanisław Maczek *(behind and between them)*

French army presenting arms to President Raczkiewicz and General Sikorski

(opposite) Polish soldiers preparing to sing at Christmas time

"Sikorski Tourists," Poles arriving in Angers to fight under Sikorski

General Sikorski and Polish soldiers exchanging Christmas greetings with traditional unleavened white bread

President Raczkiewicz and Premier Sikorski on the steps of the Polish church of Paris, Notre-Dame-de-l'Assomption, on Rue Saint Honoré, circa 1939

I had considerably neglected my book which I had begun the year before—ironically enough it dealt with a young American and his loves in the châteaux of Normandy—and I was determined that I should finish it. To do so I must leave for Normandy and quiet, and I did, but not before a minor run-in with the secret police.

Goekoop presented me to a certain Baronne Z. whom I had heard of much earlier in Warsaw, for there she had married a Swiss whom she had divorced, and yet retained his nationality as well as her own.

At Fouquet's at noon, I was having an apéritif with her and discussing a charity of inter-allied women with which she was associated. She was in the midst of telling me of the way in which she had asked the Begum Khan to head her organization, when a man came to the table, and flicked over his lapel to show the badge of the Deuxième Bureau. Immediately Baronne Z. rose and expostulated that I was not with her, the man (who later told me he should not have bothered me if she had said nothing) motioned me to follow. I had the impression that she was not surprised by this interruption. Before the mildly curious clientele, we were marched into a large Citroën with three other plainclothesmen, and after a stop at Baronne Z.'s apartment to pick up a fourth policeman, we were driven to the Ministry of the Interior opposite the Elysée and beside the Cremaillère Restaurant. The sentry was no longer the pipeclayed Garde National, but a helmeted Garde Mobile with fixed bayonet.

I had been too interested by the proceedings to admit I was an American and a journalist and had not wished to miss anything. Inside I showed my passport to the fellow who appeared to be giving the orders, and after looking at me sharply, he nodded with pleased surprise.

On his way past the guard, I noticed he flipped over his lapel again to obtain entry and said, "C'est bien Tarte Maison." Along the same line the soldiers called the Star of the Grand Cordon of the Legion of Honor the *grand crachat*, or great spittle.

Baronne Z. was left outside the inner sanctum while I was taken without delay to the chief. After displaying my papers, his attitude became solicitous and open, and he asked me how I had met the lady. I told him about Adrian and my earlier knowledge of Baronne Z. in Poland, and he scratched his head and said:

"What we don't understand is how she managed to leave Poland and cross Germany in October, and furthermore just how she is living here."

I offered with a smile that she had mentioned she was selling her jewels. The man laughed outright.

When I left, Baronne Z. was still kicking her heels in the outer office, but the next day I saw her at Fouquet's. She became voluble and showed me her vast collection of papers of every sort, diplomatic and otherwise—her husband had been of the Swiss Legation at Warsaw—and becoming visibly agitated, she confided that "they" were always after her, that the French, after her divorce, had offered her money to spy for them, and that the Poles had done the same, but she assured me that she had refused both.

After a huge luncheon to reinstate myself with the maître d'hotel who had seen me spirited away, I went to the Salon which had just opened near the Trocadéro.

With vast wonder I paraded before the paintings hung in the great "Palais" erected for the Paris Exposition. Not once did I hear an expression of approbation. On every side people shuddered and said "quelles horreures," and horrors they were, these examples of *fausse couche* art, these abortions which in reflecting the tragic deficiencies of our period point at no cure, intimate no remedy, and so tip us further into the disequilibrium which is disillusionment, into the lack of responsibility inherent in fatalism. Picasso was right when he said one could not go against nature, for nature encompasses everything, and it cannot be negated by these little daubers any more than a part become greater than the whole; yet they can distort proportion and this they have done till through their eyes one sees nothing but the rectum of nature.

How much more dangerous are the false artists than Baronne Z. It was Picasso in his statement to Christian Zervos who said the Parthenon, eclectic interpretation of nature in basic art, was a lie. I doubt whether the proletarian soul of any age would react as disfavorably before the sincere columns of the Acropolis as they did that wet afternoon in Paris before the monstrous canvases which, if taken seriously (which they must be as a disease), insult the intelligence and the senses.

Later at Madame Cutolli's in the rue de Babylone, Picasso had just hung a tempera effigy of a girl, unframed on the wall, Madame Cutolli, a Madame Faure, Kitty Goodfellow and I examined it. Kitty expressed her amusement and contempt openly, and I stirred uneasily lest someone be offended, but they must have been beyond it for condescendingly they assumed cat smiles.

"It is an attempt to portray a girl from her soul and so achieve a spiritual fourth dimension," tolerantly explained Madame Faure as if saying two and two made four. The phrase was nice. From the ceiling hung what was I believe an Arp chandelier. It was completely non-functional, bearing no lights and was composed of various balls and steel rods painted in pastel shades, the whole suspended in equipoise from a strand of piano wire. Turning to the slightest breath of wind, it was a rather fearsome thing in a mechanistic way, possessing in its perfect symmetry a restraint quite as fascinating as that which hypnotizes one's eye to the orbits of great pistons with their intimations of force in restraint of motion. Similarly, balance is imponderable and so hypnotic. But it is a common phenomenon, and when Madame Cutolli said it was basic art, I could not refrain from moving my feet restlessly on the yellow and gray of her Picasso rug, and looking about me with a curl of my lip at the disconsonance of color of her Dufys and her Laurencins and expressing my criticism perhaps more cogently, and not so basically. I interposed, "Why then is this delicate thing not painted in basic colors?"

"Ah but colors are emotion," and with a hostess' prerogative she crossed the room to another guest and I raised my eyebrows and my eyes crossed at this non-sequitur.

I remembered my friend the journalist in Vienna who had told me in 1936, "Wait, the heads will roll…the people are swilling in the pastry shops on candies and pastries. One has a craving for them when one is on edge…" These bits of frosting about me, these rugs and the "chandelier" became for me so many *éclairs* and sandwiches, and I laughed as I considered Madame Cutolli a *pâtissière* for psychopaths. But she was much more beside.

I asked her if she could get me a good Laurencin for a lady of my acquaintance. She smiled and said, "It is always women who want Laurencins. Jung would say it was an echo of the image of our masculine genes. We are all a bit Lesbian and in such a way we admit it. But the prices are all up since a painting is considered as good an investment today as anything. One can make synthetic pearls, and soon perhaps diamonds, but the world is growing away from jewels, and one will never be able synthetically to manufacture a Laurencin." Of this I was skeptical.

She had been very kind and I felt I had disturbed her in her preoccupation. I was later told that Picasso had fled into Lisbon but had there remained, though he was offered tickets to America. He was a hydrophobe and had once had to cancel a trip to England because of his fear of crossing the Channel.

Goekoop appeared five minutes after me in his sleek Delahaye at the Café de La Paix; his diplomatic immunity gave him all the gas he wanted.

We had *marennes* and a half bottle of *Champagne Nature*. And butter was brought us, as at Fouquet's, and Maxim's, inside the halves of our rolls in defiance of the regulations not permitting this delicacy. It was surreptitiously supplied us on his showing his diplomatic card—not an official prerogative—for the restaurateurs seized any opportunity, often no more than an expressed wish, to supply butter. One did not feel badly, for the reserves of dairy products were reputedly tremendous, and everyone realized the regulation against serving butter was merely to let the *permissionnaires* know that *l'arrière*, the civilian population, was sacrificing too. And soon we crossed over to attend the gala soirée at the Opéra. Debutantes were selling programs by Vertès, who was a corporal in the French Army yet spent his time in doing officer's leave clubs, as well as galas and entertainments for the men, at charity prices.

The stage represented a sector of the country a few kilometers at the rear of the Line. Two uprights supported a rod from which was hung as curtains the Tricolor and the Union Jack. An audience for this "stage on a stage" was composed of men from the French and British forces. The artistes were among those who had but lately appeared before the soldiers at the Front itself.

The evening started with the *Marseillaise*, and what British musicians term "The King," or national anthem, played on trumpets and drums with splendid effect. An announcement followed as to who was present: the President of the Republic, various members of the Diplomatic Corps and the ubiquitous Duke and Duchess of Windsor.

After the entr'acte, we managed to get backstage. We were amazed at the immensity of regions which I found not in the least tenebrous as memories of the *Phantom of the Opera* had led me to believe; yet pandemonium reigned. French *metteurs en scène* tore their hair over the lack of histrionics evinced by members of the B.E.F. and appealed for translators. Amateur performances, no matter for what purpose or on what scale, I am amused to note, retain the qualities, minus the charm of impromptus. I was amazed that all the backstage racket remained inaudible to the audience and yet it did.

Gracie Fields was introduced by Maurice Chevalier—The French, not understanding her cockney wit, gave her polite and uncomprehending applause. Our friends the British, with Gracie as the case in point, may sometimes go too far in their veneration for institutions. I overheard a French colonel say, "Elle ne présente pas l'illusion de la jeunesse!"

In leaving, I passed two Tommies staring wide-eyed at a male ballet dancer.

"Coo," they said.

Having saved a copy of the questionnaire I had submitted to Mr. William V. C. Ruxton on the *Manhattan*, I copied it, and with ramifications by Mr. Kemp and Morty Singer, I packed it together with photographs I had taken at Angers and photostats of the Polish idea of what the well-dressed ambulance driver should wear, in an envelope consigned to an official at the Hôtel Regina. He gave his assurance that the envelope would be transmitted via diplomatic pouch to the Polish Embassy at Washington which would in turn remit same to my father and Dr. Czwalenski, and in due course it was. Until the ambulances should arrive, the work of Mr. Kemp's committee was done.

En route to the Gare du Nord, I stopped off at Miss Harle's, my wondrous typist who was executing my manuscript. With her two dogs and several minor helpers, she had done much typing of the most secret documents for both the American and British Embassies in the early days and was perpetually recommended by them and Morgan's. She remembered the shelling of Paris in the last war and awaited the impending bombings with nothing short of contempt. Her French typists regarded her with awe.

I noted in my Journal:

"The relationship of the two principal allies is much that of two parents who, for purposes of social intercourse, must see one another and in so doing recognize that the other has splendid though unfamiliar qualities. Yet both are at times ineffective at making their children, the people, get along without an occasional hair-pulling or pinch, for the French still laugh covertly at Scotsmen's kilts, and the other day I saw a wretchedly uniformed French reservist, who had quite evidently drunk a glass too much, laughing and pointing at a British military policeman who strode impassively by, an expression of restrained contempt on his immaculate and composed red face. The very dress of the two men demonstrated their attitudes—for the Frenchman ill-kempt and ill-clad in a mixture of blue and khaki oddments when not on duty, would be as efficiently dressed as the Englishman immediately the necessity arose. The Britisher would imperturbably consider it a matter of pride not to change a jot in the event of his going to the Front. And I remembered the tale of one-armed, one-eyed General Carton de Wiart, V.C. (since captured in Egypt), who went over the top armed with a cane as though he were in Bond Street.

"Yet with all their ethnic differences, there is much fraternizing and mutual respect; in fact, a regulation was recently put into effect affirming that the exchange of military buttons between the French and the men of the B. E. F. must stop. I incorrectly surmised: This cooperation of extremes—that of the French and British—leading as it does to balance, has in the past proved most effective, it may again.

"In a station I observed a fully equipped Barbu for the French soldiers are now known as such rather than Poilus—a result of their cropped mustache-less beards which form a species of bristly hedge from ear to ear and in easing the chin straps of their new helmets are a tribute to the Maginot Line. (Major Guichard told me that the wind blowing through the ventilation slit separating the crest of this new helmet from its crown almost drove him mad with an eery whistling in a minor key.) As I say, I observed a Barbu laden like a donkey with a helmet on its head. His pack was of gargantuan proportions and the *gamelle*, or combination bowl and plate with which it was surmounted victoriously dominated him. The two front corners of this coat were buttoned back and his feet in immense campaign shoes were strikingly disproportionate to his thin putteed legs, yet he seemed content enough in an ineffectual way.

"Arriving at the ticket office, he fumbled for his papers in order to secure free passage. Hampered by his Lebel rifle, he gave it to his wife to hold. She was club-footed and there the poor maimed creature stood leaning on her husband's gun, patiently waiting while the strenuously equipped warrior fumbled for his *carte d'identité*—what mixtures of diurnal triviality, of domesticity, of military necessity which are the qualities of admirable, realistic France at war."

These rides out on the train were never without interest. I took a second-class ticket and automatically sat myself down in first class. It was my privilege to do so in the event of the second class being crowded and, as it invariably was, I simplified matters by going directly to first. The sole difference between the two classes lay in the fact that there were seats for six, with arms for each individual in first and communal sofas on which eight might resign themselves in second. The lights were also better in first class and it was there one was most apt to see officers, most particularly British, as it was their prerogative to travel in style.

The British landed immense quantities of materiel at Cherbourg, and every day at Bayeux, the inhabitants would align themselves along the narrow main street to observe the endless files of British trucks careen through at terrifying rates of speed. Wedged against a shop front, the hubs grazing me by a foot or more, the Tommies waving at the pretty girls, I felt one of these monstrous machines might plow through the entire town should it skid on a wet cobble. The Route Nationale, Number 13, paralleled the railroad to Paris and it was a wonder to me the railway lines, leading from Cherbourg through Bayeux, Caen, Evreux and Mantes to the Gare St. Lazare in Paris were not bombed before they were, since Cherbourg, Evreux, Caen and Mantes were cities including military objectives of the first order, subject to disruption were the common lines of communication severed.

My train was held up at Caen while a sailor remonstrated to a military police captain that the guard had been impolite in evicting him from first class. He had been in my compartment. When he left, the Frenchman opposite affirmed that the sailor "avait fait dans sa culotte." Though seated beside him, I had not been aware that he was particularly malodorous, yet the French in being realists are perpetually on the lookout for that sort of thing, and sensitive to the humor of the biologic. I was much impressed with the generous attitude of the officer toward the vociferating (and drunken) sailor. In England the man would have been clapped into a dungeon, but in England a private would not be in a first-class carriage, and if he were would have contained himself. The English people have never razed their palaces, and the French are for the most part unimpressed with tradition, and when in fine company or glittering surroundings, they remember the Tuileries and are inclined to hitch up their belts. Patriotism is tradition to a certain extent, and so I mused and slept.

There was no regular *wagon* restaurant, but a wagon buffet which served a *plat du jour* if one were fortunate enough to get a seat. Around the bar was a mass of soldiers drinking beer and vociferating, while the dimmed passage-ways were crammed with people seated on their luggage or sleeping stertorously with their heads on one another's feet. Progress was slow, and in the course of many journeys I learned to adapt myself to these conditions. To my surprise I recognized the steward, an oldish man with gray hair. He had been the *wagons-lits* man on the North Express two years before and of tremendous assistance in getting some shotguns I had with me through Germany into Poland. These fellows were always remarkable, and ambassadors in their own right, for they knew several languages and all the officials at the various frontiers throughout Europe. In short, they belonged to the Free Masonry of Cook's men, bank commissionaires and hotel concierges—a shrewd and to be respected lot.

By a miracle, he recognized me or said he did, which was worth the same amount to him—and I asked him why he was there. He looked down at his once dapper brown uniform with its "WL" at the collar and half the crested silver buttons torn off, a plate of ragoût dripping gravy in either hand, and answered in flawless English: "It's all they find me useful for." As he went away I knew that he was thinking of the *Train Bleu* clicking over the frontiers of Europe with a Louis XV mirrored private car at the rear; of fat tips in pounds and dollars, florins and rubles.

"Je vous en remercie, Monsieur," he said, bowing low as I left and I felt very much like bowing back.

"Quinze ragoûts, chef!" I heard him shout as I stumbled through the hallways hoping some woman, feigning pregnancy, had not taken my seat. Others had no more rights than the men.

I had wired ahead to the Citroën garage to send good Leloup with the Commerciale which had been returned to us when the Red Cross lost interest in our district as a result of the cold. He met me at the wintry station, and I had many talks with him on the trips during which I returned him to his little brick house before driving on to the Abbaye. Once he informed me he had been in the antiaircraft during the last war, and that the average number of shells fired by a good gun crew to bring down one plane was five thousand—to me a preposterous number till I saw them near Sézanne pocketing the air with black shrapnel smoke so continuously, with such a fierce rhythm, and with so little effect.

Jeanne, the maid who had had so many run-ins with the Mayor, had given birth to a baby a month before and brought the infant with her. One by one, because of the child, I relieved her of her duties which were at most light, until she did nothing but ferment my meals in her kitchen, more or less at the hours it pleased her, and make my bed. Another woman came in once a week to do the cleaning. Despite the idiosyncrasies attendant upon her new-found maternity, and her refrain with gestures, "Que ses seins lui tirait," I liked Jeanne and we got along very well in the sense that she never disturbed me and since eating alone with nothing to watch or no one to talk to bores me intolerably, my meals were very simple.

I dislike the sound of chewing.

Twice a week, when the butcher shops were open I would pass the open front of my particular one where were suspended flayed oxen reminiscent of Rembrandt, their diaphragms tastefully cut into designs by the butcher's assistant; I would make a sign with my finger and on returning thirty minutes later I would be given six chops, a large rump steak cut in two equal segments to serve twice and a roast of veal.

The pastry shop was forced by decree to be shut most of the week, the *pâtissière* told me, and her tears rolled down the end of her nose into her *éclairs* and *bostocks*. These poor people will be more affected than the butchers and with them will pass much of the gaiety of France. One can tolerate one's self setting up a reserve of meat in wartime but not of cakes. The poor woman sold only what could be eaten on the days her shop was open while the butchers, despite being forced to shut the greater part of the week, sold as much as ever they did. I purchased a large supply of chocolate bars which I inadvertently dedicated to the rats by placing in a cupboard of my little salon. The damp cold of Winter forced me to spend all my time in the one room except when I retired to sleep or went for a walk in the afternoon on the *falaise* or visited some friend in the environs.

There had been no such cold in Normandy for over a century. Never before in the memory of man had the streams and *viviers* been so thick with ice, the Curé informed me. He had received me in his one "warm room." He sat in a dilapidated *bergère*—the invention of a king's mistress so tradition holds—his feet on a stack of newspapers and I thought of the great piles of mine in Paris. On his shelves were rows of confiscated novels, of Latin primers and works by the hack-writers for the Catholic Church.

Monsieur le Curé told me the morale was good and asked me news of Paris. Soon I followed him out into his dejected garden past his rusted woman's bicycle leaning against the wall to the church, damp and bitterly cold and with but an intimation of incense. He changed the candle in the *veilleuse* placed on the altar the day war was declared. I thought of the little monument with the twenty-five names of the glorious dead in the village square and of the Summer Feast of St. Lawrence's Day when the brazen-helmeted firemen, slightly tipsy, were wont to stand at attention the Mayor deposited a little wreath at its foot. In many cases the names of the sons may be added to those of their fathers if there is room enough. Monsieur le Curé would keep his flame burning till his flock had returned, and I left him, his gnarled hands joined in a prayer for his dispersed flock, and blue from a cold to which he seemed insensible.

One afternoon when on my weekly shopping, I met Daisy de Broglie and she told me she had received sums from various Franco-American societies in the United States, but that they were losing interest...that in addition the five thousand francs which had been sent were not enough to erect anything permanent but unless something permanent was established she felt any giving would be desultory (a result quite understandable since donors want something definitely theirs to support, something with which they might be identified, and of which they might possess photographs). I suggested we have something to warm us, and we went to the *estaminet*. To my amazement I saw a bottle of whiskey on the shelf and ordered two whiskies and water. Solemnly the young lady in attendance brought over two *limonade* glasses which she filled to the brim with whiskey after setting beside our glasses small tumblers filled with water.

"Who taught you to make this drink, Mademoiselle?"

"The Tommies, Monsieur!" she solemnly said, then blushed and smiled, lowering her head with a giggle.

We drank the whiskey and water in proportions inverse to those usually served and were much warmed thereby.

Daisy took me over to her *oeuvre* which was a little hospital for sick refugee children. There Isabelle Foy was on duty with several Sisters of a nursing order, engaged in tending the children ill with measles, cold, chicken pox, and mixtures thereof.

I asked Daisy why she didn't spend the 5000 francs on her *oeuvre* and call it the *Oeuvre* of the Franco-American Society. She answered that the Government which in fact supported her little hospital would never permit such a step.

Nevertheless, I had a sign painted and writing paper emblazoned with red crosses and a title, "Oeuvre of the Franco-American Society," and Daisy and I suspended the sign over the entrance which I photographed with the nuns standing beneath—I had great difficulty in overcoming their modesty and they blushed and arranged their coiffes much in the manner of their more worldly sisters. As soon as the pictures were taken, the sign was taken down and stored away. The Franco-American Society was delighted with their *oeuvre* which they in part supported, the children benefited immensely from the little deception we had practiced, for the funds rolled in as a result of the photographs and the feeling that the Americans had something definite to which they might contribute—while the French Government unknowingly benefited directly.

Daisy informed me her husband, Prince Joseph de Broglie, had been against his will made a first lieutenant—which he resented because it was in actuality no more important than a second lieutenant but with seven times the work since he was his captain's executive—and yet Daisy had more work than both. Among her most difficult tasks was that of getting blood from the peasants. Intensely xenophobe, they were very wary of submitting themselves to the necessary punctures or even to receive the preliminary blood tests to ascertain to what blood group they might belong. Yet Daisy understood their mentality wonderfully well and had an astonishing success, explaining with great care and sufficient lucidity just what she was about. The syringes she covered with knitted blue coats, perhaps not quite sanitary yet one could not see the blood rising within.

One night I went over to Lison, a small town on the Cherbourg-Paris lines where troop trains, as often as not laden with Tommies, stopped to get something to eat from an S. S. B. M. canteen run by Daisy and others suitably arrayed in the blue-and-white trained-nurse dresses of their service, the Societé de Secours pour Blessés Militaires.

It was an all-night job, since the trains came in uneven waves filling the little building with hordes of soldiers and sailors. The building constructed for the purpose by a competent architect reserve officer included rough but serviceable bunks and a lavatory at one end, a kitchen at the other and a bar and dining room at the middle.

It was operated on a "break-even" basis, the soldiers paying five francs for a meal consisting in soup, fish or eggs, meat and potatoes, and white or red wine, as well as bread and the best butter I have tasted. The helpings were Pantagruelian.

Two in number were the nurses who took charge each night. Fourteen in all, each came one night of the week. The work began at five in the afternoon, and they might leave for home at seven the next morning. Daisy said the English Tommies invariably called out to her "a cup of tea, Sweetheart," and often gave her as much as a twenty-franc tip.

When a troop train did pass through, as many as two or three hundred men had to be served—and quickly. On such an occasion I was impressed as barman, and engaged myself in passing beer, wine and coffee over the counter.

In the middle of the evening when we were all occupied with five cups in either hand, a state of alerte was declared and all the lights went out. Work was carried on by the flame of one candle, as conversation continued and the anti-aircraft went off every once in a while, and all the accounts balanced the next morning.

The chief subject of discussion was the relative merit of the weapons or branches in which the various soldiers served.

The next day I noted somewhat confusedly in my Journal, yet with emotion, when I called on Daisy that "she'd been up all night the night before as is her custom twice a week, tending a counter at a station restaurant for troops which came in recurrent waves to beat on her nerves throughout the night. Bearded and smelling of Caporal tobacco and wine, tired and shouting to make themselves heard above the escaping steam of the locomotives, haggard under the blue light of the Défense Passive, their hobnails restless and grating on the cement quais…as she spoke cheerfully of her vigils at Lison my glance traveled from her face to the window and down the vistas of Balleroy Park, the shadows of the plane trees and lindens oblique with the rays of the Lorrainesque sun, down to a group of hunters emerging from the woods. These were *permissionnaires* since they alone are permitted to shoot, and I thought of her daytime occupations, of her work among infant refugees. The war threatens intimate pleasure as it does the very existence of children. Neither is of use without the other."

Jean Cabestan perpetually repeated to me with a wonderful gesture (that of pulling in his chin and shutting his eyes with his arms stretched rigidly at either side, his fists shut in confirmation of the French maxim that to sleep well one sleeps with closed fists), that everyone was sleeping at the Quai d'Orsai. In exasperation with inactivity he had come up to visit me, though I had advised him there should be nothing to do at Longues.

Yet he came.

On driving him back from the station, I heard a man's voice from the window of the one refugee left to us at the Abbaye, a Polish woman who had occupied rooms over the *pressoir*, our ancient cider press, since September. I called to Philippe, our gardener, who loathed the woman, to ask to whom the voice belonged. He answered with restrained irony it was the "husband" of the refugee.

She had come and as I have noted elsewhere, been imposed on us by the system of allocations. She had brought with her a five-year-old child by an individual whom she planned, she virtuously advised me, to marry the next summer. Thoroughly unpleasant, though always neat and clean, she had found it to be to her advantage in life to admit satisfaction with nothing. The gardener claimed she stole from his supply of firewood, the maid that she sold herself in the village, and both that she interfered with their work by her borrowings of their possessions. Furthermore, they were secretly annoyed at her promenadings in the garden hand in hand with her son, in the manner of a "grande dame." She had ingratiated herself with the Mayor by doing much gratuitous sewing, at which she was an expert, for his wife and had overcharged Mrs. Long and Madame Guichard for work they had given her from motives of kindness. There was no reason apparent that the woman should stay on when all the others had left, with the exception of orphans and the violently poor, which last she was not, for she sported ugly diamond earrings and like finery in the pierced lobes of her ears.

I might have let the matter pass, but Cabestan urged me to ask Philippe if he had given permission to the man to enter the place. I did, and Philippe had not.

This revelation annoyed me, and the man was called down that I might see what he looked like. On his presenting himself before us in a surly manner I asked him what he was doing on the property without due permission of entry. His answer was self assured; that he had secured permission from the Mayor. I admonished him to the effect that the Mayor was in no position to give an individual such a right unless he were a refugee duly allocated with my collaboration to the property. The man, a species of intelligent rat, seemed unimpressed. Philippe was looking on stolidly, but I saw a tightening of his jaw, and he shifted his spade from one hand to the other.

Quite suddenly, in staccato German, Cabestan told the fellow to remove his hands from his pockets.

Startled he turned and said, his voice pitched high, that he did not understand.

Cabestan, much the Inquisitor, repeated his order in Russian and the man took his hands from his pockets and crossed them somewhat lamely as in subject defiance over his chest. I did not enjoy this exhibition, as no republican would. I was later made to appreciate the justice of Cabestan's actions. We have perhaps too much respect for the sanctity of equality and it is known we have too much heart, or perhaps a better word would be sentimentality.

"Your papers," ordered Cabestan and the man gave them over. By now, the woman had rejoined us, and the man told her to go to the Mayor. I would have interfered, but Cabestan said in English, "Do let her go."

We left the man in the car vociferating with Philippe, and we retreated to the living room to examine his papers.

"As I thought," said Jean, "the man is a Russian, but he seems to have a job as a mechanic in a factory. Hum. He arrived in France in 1935—*Le Front Populaire*—and he has no right to be here, since he should be in Paris. We shall call the police."

The Brigadiers from Port-en-Bessin were summoned.

In the meanwhile, the Mayor had returned with the woman and blustered about until Jean showed him his Foreign Office card which by virtue of the French hierarchy gave him power over the Mayor. The fellow subsided, particularly when Cabestan remarked that he noticed the Russian's papers were not in order. Out of kindness to me, he did not charge the Mayor with incompetency or worse in allowing the man to go about without permission from the Police in Paris, for he knew that I should have to get along with the village authorities till spring. Soon the Mayor left, discomfited, and the police arrived on their bicycles with their brief cases familiarly strapped over the cross-bar.

"See, my son is crying," said the Russian. But the little boy was evidently enjoying himself for he was grinning from one ear to the other. This appeal to our sympathy amused the police, and without further ado, they said "aliens," and gave the Russian a push, adding that it was a pity he didn't have his mother to sell for his liberty.

These splendid fellows, the gendarmes, deserve a parenthesis for they're the caliber Napoleon conscripted as non-commissioned officers in his grenadier guard; they're the type which occasionally produces a Murat; they are those among whom the Emperor was proud to wear the woolen epaulet.

We had a glass of Calvados together, and the Brigadier-Chef said that France was too good, that she was too hospitable and that such guests should be placed on a highway leading to the East and told not to return...and he was right, for this Russian was of the type of petty "agent provocateur," the saboteur who will drop a nail among intricate gears, a match in a corn crib. He was hustled off, and the woman left of her own accord soon after. I was glad to see them go, and the next day Philippe was whistling, and Jeanne as well, and both were very deferential to Jean who lectured me for having made a display of bourgeois soft-heartedness in much the following manner:

"Normandy is the last province of France to welcome Communism. Didn't the famed Chouans—immortalized by Barby d'Aurevilly—as the result of their attacks against the Revolutionaries some one hundred and fifty years ago cause the Republic to level all the trees of the Bessin which stood within musket range of the road? Is not the Senator of Calvados, Monsieur le Comte d'Harcourt, is not the deputy his nephew, the Duc? And this *canaille* comes to pollute the region with their Marxism, their thefts and shifting eyes."

And in a more serious vein he added that France was in the most dire peril from the inner gnawings of such pollution and America itself; it was folly to be weak and to release a father because the child smiled, to be kind where kindness was not understood but considered weakness.

The next day Jeanne told me that the refugee, on Jeanne's receiving a small check from my parents, at the birth of her son had said, "They don't do it for you but for themselves."

The next day I drove Cabestan over to Port-en-Bessin to pay my respects to the Chief of Police and to show off the harbor.

On the hill above arises an ancient stone barbican erected by Vauban and pierced with cannon ports. The inner basin is sheltered by long-cut stone moles stretching granite arms to wrest a bit of stillness from the moving sea. Yet it remained rough enough for the Bishop to become seasick in blessing the deck of a fishing smack some weeks before. At the time I remember idly wondering what he would do with his mitre. We arrived to witness two large fishing boats put out to sea. Propelled through the inner basin by powerful diesels, the exhausts emitting a rhythmic chugging, the bluff craft had triangles of oily canvas set at either mast, I assumed to increase their stability by the wind. Their crews are noted for braving the elements, yet in addition there was a not remote possibility of strafings by Heinkels with but little protection afforded under wooden decks.

As the first of the little ships stopped for the swinging bridge to be pivoted to one side, I observed the cross set at the masthead vibrating to the pulsations of the diesel auxiliary. Beside me a red-nosed sea-dog told me she was the *Sainte-Anne*, that she had brought in a mine about a meter in diameter a week before which proved on examination to be a French one of the war of 1914!

Two other sailors who were dressed in blue canvas rather than the more familiar red of the Breton fishermen, told of their experiences in German prison camps in 1915; of the bread made from straw they were given to eat and of the sadism of their guards. I had heard much the same from Philippe the gardener who was captured in the first month of the last war—when the French wore red trousers and went helmetless—and he had passed four years in the salt mines of Germany where a sentry had broken his arm with the butt of a rifle. If the youth could harbor the hate these men evinced in their memories, I felt little fear for France. The anger in reminiscence of the smaller sailorman was as much a part of him as the leg left him by the war.

We passed fishermen's wives mending nets and by them children casting stones into the sea. I left thinking of happier times.

Hubert, Fido's brother, was *en permission*, and came to visit Jean and me his last evening at Longues. Tall and slim, he was a perfect picture of what a cavalryman should be, though his spurs were an irony since his regiment was motorized. In June, he was to be of the Southern-most of the columns "five kilometers long" which were prepared at a moment's notice, alas too rapidly as it proved, to penetrate into Belgium.

It has been written too many times to bear much repetition here, how these columns, on entering Belgium, met with hordes of refugees spurred in their flight by the wild tales of fifth columnists; of how the columns and the refugees authentic and provocateurs became entangled on the roads, and of the Panzer divisions driving their salients between and thus infilading roads quivering under Stuka attack.

In early May, Miss Anne Morgan had said that I might go to visit her *oeuvre* near Belgium. I encountered much greater difficulty in securing permission than I expected because it was explained the French were busily occupied in constructing casemates and giving tardy evidence they realized their weakness in not having extended the Line. The choice to advance into Belgium rather than to form a solid front at the border was, as has been reiterated, the great blunder of the French General Staff. Had the Maginot Line, whose creator was canonized during the Winter months, not stopped short at Sedan it might well have kept out the Germans. Had the French stayed in France along their frontier and not proceeded into Belgium in response to the equivocal cry of Leopold, the war should not at any event have been brought to so rapid a conclusion. But such surmise is futile.

Three days before Belgium fell, I had an apéritif with Thérèse de Caraman-Chimay. She had all but been captured by the Germans to the North. A great friend of Prince Charles, Leopold's brother,

she was much distressed at accounts to the effect that he had lost a leg near Sedan. She wished to go to his side, a course from which I hoped to dissuade her, yet she asked me how to secure the proper permissions....She was very tired, and we sat at the café table set in the street opposite the Hôtel George V. In a monotone she reminisced that Charles disliked the King, for Leopold was jealous of his unconventional and charming brother and made a practice of sending him off to be Governor of the Congo or on some other royal but uninteresting job. One day, she stood beside Charles at a window watching Leopold caracole on a white horse. As the Palladin King passed to the acclamation of the crowds, she turned her head to Prince Charles and with enthusiasm said, "But you know, he is magnificent!" Prince Charles answered, "Yes, but wait till he's up against something; you'll see him better." Three days after telling me this story she did.

Hubert was among those who were evacuated at Dunkirk; the ship on which he left the coast was struck by a bomb. He was rescued by a British yacht, perhaps the *Greyhound*, to be taken to England and reshipped immediately to Brest from whence he traveled to Evreux to meet the German Armies which had crossed the Seine. Incorporated into the Army of the Loire, he was taken prisoner but released after ten days, and demobilized.

As we sat about the fire, he, Jean and I, to warm ourselves with peach Bolas cupped in our hands, the wind drove against the window in fitful gusts, the smoke occasionally purling back into the dimly lighted chamber. I looked at the faces of my two friends, their lips touching the rim of the glasses held before them. First Hubert: having begun his military service as a private, I remembered he had passed up the ranks of the intricate hierarchy of the French non-commissioned officers to the achievements of three-bar sergeant—a post usually held by the professional alone—Hubert who had a letter in his pocket from his general recommending him for a lieutenant's commission. Then on the other side, Jean, a bit older, so Voltarian, and so keen. Both so dissimilar and yet such good fellows in their mutual respect, both doing their duty to the utmost, yet with a certain cynicism as evidence of unrest. I felt apart from them, yet if I were beside them now I feel we should be bound by straighter ties.

Hubert chatted of a training mishap of the week before—in a *chenillette*, or unarmed light tank less than four feet high, fast and designed to carry munitions and haul anti-tank guns, he had gone at a hill with a novice. Frightened at taking it head on, the inexperienced driver had swerved at the last moment and the tank had upset. Quickly Hubert dragged him out, ran a few steps away and prostrated himself on the ground. The *chenillette* had been laden with mines.

Fido later told me Hubert had given up his bed to one of his young soldiers who was cold from prolonged exposure. He was a fine officer.

There is no doubt that in wartime the most enviable place to be is in the Government—not from motives of personal safety since all suffer very much alike as statistics have shown, but rather because the Government protects her own (if one is not too important) in disavowing the Army when the fighting is done. So many friends wondered what the future held for them and knew France should be ruined when the bugles, swathed in the tricolor of victory or crepe of national obsequies, had blown the "cease fire."

"You know," said Hubert, with a shake of his head, "every time I see my relations such as aunts I feel their minds are filled with thoughts of mortuary wreaths when they look on me; of candles and coffins and of what they shall wear at the funeral, and of meters of black crepe and black hat pins stuck through their hair."

He told an unpleasant story of two women sitting in a café at which he had his table. They spoke in English, and in casual French fashion which is a national prerogative, he eavesdropped. A young soldier came up and paid his respects, but on being coldly received, went away.

The woman said: "I was nice to *him* when the war began and he said he was going to the front because I hadn't expected to see him again…"

Hubert had turned, and to their surprise asked if they resented the fellow's not being killed.

He leaned back and emptied his glass and filled it again from the bottle at his side.

Jean said in exhaling the smoke from his cigarette that his aunt has been angry at his sister for the latter's not knowing her father's citations.…Our silences were evidence of the nostalgia we felt for peace and the past.

Hubert asked me of the neighbors who had rented half their château to the rich refugees. I told him they were all dressed in black—a trio of nice yet essentially unesthetic girls save for the youngest with corn-yellow hair and haunting Celtic eyes. All women in common with the mad-dog of the Bible, we agreed, are blessed with one good trait, organ or feature at the least. For all of us I threw my glass into the fire.

Cabestan, like an Arouet on a bicycle, pedaled from Paris to Bordeaux, leaving the capital on June 12th. He is now at Wiesbaden on the Commission de Paix, sitting behind his desk with his thick spectacles perched on his arched nose quite as if nothing had happened. Hubert is demobilized and kicking stones dejectedly in the road.

Hubert had told me of his Russian brother-in-law Anitchkoff, who though not French had been mobilized by special decree with all white Russians who had accepted the hospitality of France for a specified number of years. Had he been a week older he would have been over thirty-five and so not affected and everyone was much amused at his mock wrath, amused in the way one is at another who has lost in the horse race, or had his hat blown off or a chamber pot emptied on his head.

Anitchkoff was in the infantry but was later transferred because the varicose veins he had acquired in the ball rooms of Paris interfered with his marchings. He objected strenuously to being addressed in the familiar thee and thou by his officers, their unofficial prerogative. Often *en permission*, over his wine he threatened to retort in similar terms, an action technically permissible (though unthinkable in practice) in the Armies of the Republic. His French wife placated him. Anitchkoff in common with all those belonging to territorial regiments was dressed in the odds and ends of the last war. He showed me holes patched in his trousers and in his utter disgust said they were bullet holes, that he was dressed in the coat a man had been shot in. Once in Paris he was visiting his father-in-law, Major Guichard, when a colonel entered.

"Thou art the orderly?"

Anitchkoff drawing himself up: "No, the son-in-law." The Colonel discomfited: "Oh, I beg your pardon, Sir."

There were many anomalies in this Citizen army, anomalies derided in Maurice Chevalier's *Paris-Londres* at the Folies-Bergères. The words of his song were to the effect that the officers and men were of the most disparate creeds and occupations as well as political parties, yet were welded into a fine army....

At certain dinner tables one might see a general seated opposite a private, yet privates and non-coms were not permitted into the better restaurants. For this reason I had friends who, being sergeants, had their bars sewed almost straight as an officer's rather than slanted in order to get into Maxim's. In any event their uniforms were magnificent, *uniformes de fantaisie*, with spurs and boots, chechias and Spahi capes and the head waiters bowed low on their arrival, not daring believe, or perhaps winking at the fact these splendid Mars-like apparitions were but corporals.

Hubert said his other brother-in-law, Ste. Marie, a subaltern of infantry, had seen some action, that he had been in a house and defended it against a grenade attack. Later when I saw his eighteen-year-old wife, Doudouce, she spoke of the event with a calm and unaffected courage which gave me much to think on. The extended periods of the war gave one time to weigh trivial incidents and their significance yet the truth, a tragic culmination would make so evident, remained unobserved.

The French Army was officered by its regular career officers as well as by those who having taken certain examinations, as law, were qualified if they were not too old to enter an officer's training school. Such were Fido and my cousin, Tony de Morès, whose father, the Due de Vallambrosa, had been at Verdun for four years during the last war and was once again in uniform despite ill health. Tony said, to his amazement, much more attention was devoted to instructions regarding how to fold one's kit rather than how to fight. The training camps were grim and for the first three months of the six-month course they lived in wretched surroundings infested with bedbugs, washing down their own floors and cleaning out the latrines. For this work Fido used a gas mask. Their work was most exhausting though the food was good and the wine laden with *bromures* or bromides. The dangers of syphilis and gonorrhea were graphically displayed to the men in moving pictures so horrible that soldiers often fainted. How effective such deterrents were, I do not know.

On graduating, one became an aspirant, or cadet lieutenant, having the duties but not the pay of a second lieutenant—a ruse of the Government. This rank lasted indefinitely, and was the rank I later held in the Polish Army.

If one were a doctor or dentist or pharmacist or veterinary, one became automatically an officer, though the color of one's kepi, scarlet, purple, dark blue or green respectively, denoted to what arm one belonged—and received but vague salutes from the men.

Undoubtedly there were some injustices and stupidities, to wit, one friend whom I found sleeping on hay in a garage one block from his home to which military discipline forbade him to return for the night. During the last war, at the age of twenty he had served as an interpreter with the rank of second lieutenant. With so many others who have since been so cruelly disillusioned, he believed there would never be another war and did no military periods. As a result, when the war did come, he was drafted as a private and despite speaking perfect English, he was employed as a *rond-de-cuire*, or circle of leather, as the functionaries are called from the circle of leather they wear about their wrists to protect their cuffs from wear and tear and ink stains, doing the same sort of work as our cook's uneducated husband.

The position of interpreter was much coveted and one friend, Pierre de Douville, knew the captain who had access to the files containing the applications of those who wished to serve as liaison officers with the B. E. F. A certain officer was to consider the huge pile among which Pierre knew his to be. At his urging, the captain took Pierre's application and put it at the top. Until the day he was assigned to his duties, billeting and regimental liaison, Pierre was on a fever lest the officer had started at the bottom.

The English lived high and the fact that their privates were paid some eighty times as much as the French (who received fifty centimes per day or ten francs when in the line) was deeply resented—most particularly since the French were fully mobilized and the English but playing at it as at the first of World War I. "It's unfair," a friend remarked, "They get all the wine and all the women—

there'll not be a bottle of champagne or a virgin in France after they've left!" Which was pretty much what the German propaganda hoped to make one think. Certainly, there were many petty frictions, and there is little doubt the British phlegm—which might well be interpreted by any normal human being as an assumption of superiority—was found to be annoying, I remember at the Chambrun's I was seated opposite a Commander Howard of the "Wavy Navy," I had just mentioned the word "tradition," and catching at it, he said, "Have you tradition in America?" I was inspired to retort, "You will soon be appealing to our tradition to help you out of the messes you get into," but did not from deference to the French.

Yet all in all, the British rank and file, of whom one did not see many in Paris were popular enough...it was carefully explained the men were not allowed more than twelve hours leave in the capital, this rather than let one assume there were not many in France to be seen. I noted:

"I walked from the rue de Talleyrand to my apartment near the Etoile and on the Champs Elysées remarked children proudly being led astride the red-tasseled hired donkeys. Nearby men were occupied in the construction of a bombproof shelter, so near that the donkeys trampled the newly turned earth. What a chiaroscuro! And British Tommies were chatting with the children and their trim *bonnes*. I've noticed the British military police one sees about to be exceptionally tall men. Their physiques, scarlet armbands and lanyarded pistols attract the admiration and stares of men and women alike. The French are pleased with the British, and sometimes remind me of a small boy showing off his big brother to a pugnacious contemporary with a 'See! I told you so!' and a jeer. They glow with pride at the British Naval victories."

Undoubtedly, few people mind being mistaken for English.

Fido, Hubert, Jean Cabestan and I motored over to see the Vicomte de Douville-Maillefeu, father to Mano and Pierre.

He was kind enough to show us about the park and indicated with pride a large amount of wood he'd felled. It lay about on the ground, preparatory to being cut to proper lengths and taken into the house. By the seaside, he had a potato patch. His farmer named Pestle (un des plus vieux noms du pays!) tended 45 hectares of land, in addition to other work. If the young had done their part as well as the old....

We helped carry in the wood, and later Mano and I had our photographs taken standing before a Nazi flag and I put on one of the German hats—I assumed a stationmaster's—surmounted with a black button and having green ear muffs at the side. We decided it was very bourgeois and inoffensive. Mano's sister was there and we had tea and she talked of her husband who had but just become a captain in the Chasseurs Alpins. She was immensely proud of her "blue devil."

It is strange to write of this period on which nothing happened and one but prepared half-heartedly for eventualities one could but barely discern in the tenebrous future. One's friends came and went all very much alike in their khaki and their tales of eating vast sides of beef while we civilians for their benefit mockingly drew in our belts and assumed hang-dog expressions. One visited châteaux and lovely country houses one had known so well in the past, tall windows and shaded lawns, terraces set with green iron chairs and tables and red-and-white parasols, and teas of sirop and madeleines and the swimming and the hide-and-seek as children in the laurel leaves of the parks. And now all this was changed, yet the minds of people not changed—the parks were littered with fallen trees, the men and boys were in rough brown cloth, yet this war was a game—it did not signify, it was but an interruption, and we felt that which we had known so well could not and would never change.

In June, I carried an elderly soldier in my ambulance. I discovered he had convalesced in the Douville's garden in 1918.

Soon I returned to Paris to see Miss Harle, my typist, to lunch with Krakowski at the Interallié on the occasion of presenting him with my article on Mieckiewicz. I mentioned that I was to have tea with Monsieur Fäy who is now at the head of the Bibliotèque Nationale. Cabestan pursed his lips and lowered his eyes and I desisted. It appeared that Krakowski and Fäy who were of different political colorings disliked another all the more intensely in that both were intellectuals. The same relationship existed between Fäy and Mowrer. If it were not jealousy which prompted them, I was decided to have lower opinions of all three.

I arrived early at the great buff hôtel in the Quartier St. Germain and clicked up the uncarpeted stairway to Monsieur Fäy's salon situated near the apartments of the Comtesse de Fels and Monsieur Alexis Léger of the French Foreign Office. Many people came—a woman with lithographs illustrating one of Rimbaud's poems; Laval's daughter, the Comtesse de Chambrun; Monsieur Abel Bonnard of the Academy, seated on the corner of a table, a glass cupped in his hand and his hair white or rather silver, brushed about his small, well-shaped head much as an aureole, and he spoke in dialectic flashes of extraordinary wit. The Comte Etienne de Beaumont, a Charlus as Proust described Montesquiou-Fezensac, a splendid arrogant voice, yet a mincing virtuosity of speech. He and Fäy had organized a rolling library for the Army. All these were of the intellectual Right, the gadfly of the Government. I was told that Madame de Crussol, Daladier's mistress who had derived her fortune from her father's sardines, was limned as "La Sardine qui s'est crue Sole." Later, when Daladier suffered from a sprain incurred in falling from his horse and was confined to his quarters, the cognoscenti reported he had attempted to pinch the Marquise on hers while at the gallop.

Cabestan, who had turned up, regaled Madame de Chambrun with tales of his trips through Russia in third-class compartments, his hikes in Czechoslovakia with Riancourt, a friend I had been at school with in Switzerland, who was noted for his strength. I can imagine them both; Jean with the assurance which, though not a trait of character, he might assume as an effective weapon to supplement his perfect knowledge, and the burly Riancourt who might kick down a door or bash in someone's head with his fist if need be—the perfect pair for a fact-finding tour. It is the diplomacy we do not understand, that of sending a linguist to gauge the temper of a people in the intimate byways which lead to the nexus of political unrest. Yet it was I, Madame de Chambrun asked to dinner.

I noted:

"Concerning Mr. Welles, who is now in Germany, but expects to be at the Crillon near the American Embassy and Elysée Palace within the next two or three days, there exist two schools of thought; e.g., those idealistically inclined, believe the result of his impartial study may lead to an ultimate solution. The second group, who might bear the charge of worldliness with a shrug, consider the entire affair as motivated by politics. A few individuals are convinced that there may be truth in both suppositions, and in my hearing it was said by an unofficial personage that he considered it wretchedly bad manners for Roosevelt to send his little boy visiting at such a busy time!"

I had a letter to General Adalbert de Chambrun who knew much of American politics. His talented wife is the daughter of the late Speaker of the House of Representatives, Nicholas Longworth. On my mentioning that I was on the *Chicago Daily News* he told me a tale of its great rival the *Tribune* which had once run an article to the effect that the French were disinterring the remains of the American dead because the U.S. Government had not paid the rent for the cemeteries. The story was, of course, entirely false, and the General, on arriving in Chicago said as much to Colonel McCormick, the owner of the *Tribune*. Furthermore, since they had made speeches together at the dedications of various Franco-American war monuments, the General taxed the Colonel with the knowledge that any such talk was gross and perhaps knowing error.

The Colonel with tears in his eyes, according to the General, avowed what the General said to be the truth and affirmed that the American press in being unsubsidized as in France, was forced to run such articles from time to time to increase circulation.

That evening at the General's son's apartment everyone was in a festive mood since our host "avait fait son Jockey." Madame de Chambrun, the General's wife, was very kind and I spoke to her of my novel and the difficulties of composition, not realizing that she was an authoress seventeen times over. Nevertheless, she kindly asked me to lunch later at her apartment. There I was to see a painting of Napoleon executed by one among David's pupils who labored over sketches to be incorporated into their master's great canvases. On the reverse side David had graciously remarked that the resemblance was the most perfect to come from his atelier. The color of the Emperor's hair was evident, a deep auburn, and later Thérèse de Caraman-Chimay, who possessed a lock, said that such it was.

Dominated by the Emperor, I sat opposite the Senator de Chambrun, the brother of the General. Later when his was the solitary dissident vote cast against the dissolution of the parliaments, it was circulated he had not heard the subject for voting. This unkind interpretation was plausible since I remembered the old gentleman was deaf.

And then one day, I noted:

"It has frozen thrice and now the days are warm and of some mornings an overcoat is not necessary to comfort. The birds blithely sing and the philatelists have resumed their bi-weekly meetings near the Ambassadeurs, displaying and exchanging stamps, chatting and wandering between the green iron tables set under the leafless trees of the Champs Elysées."

Yes, it was warming once again and all the world rejoiced that one of their predictions, Spring, had come to pass. I was no longer forced to bathe twice a day like the Japanese to keep the heat in my veins on the Mondays, Tuesdays, and Wednesdays one was allowed warm water; I might leave the balcony window open and enjoy walking in the streets and throwing the crumbs left over from my morning's *croissant* to the pigeons near the Etoile.

Mr. Douglas MacArthur of the American Embassy and Mr. Shoop had put me up for the American Club, and on the Thursday meetings at lunch in the Interallié I had the privilege of hearing many men of note, yet none foretold the future. Among the best were Jules Romains, and earlier in the year, Giraudoux. The latter was much criticized for the inefficient way he ran the Ministry of Information and was eventually superseded. Yet that he was an artist was evident to his advantage in his speech. His son with whom I had lunch on several occasions was but twenty and had aroused considerable jealousy at the Quai d'Orsai since his father often sent him on missions to England. Tall and looking like a dissolute Apollo, dissolute from too much thought and the pallor of a hurried adolescence, he was an Anglophile and probably well suited temperamentally for his missions. His translations of his father's plays had a certain vogue in London. But what the father lacked in system, there is no doubt the son lacked in years. Certainly he was much appreciated in London, perhaps too much.

On Washington's birthday, in the Grand Ballroom of the Grand Hôtel, Daladier was to speak before the club, but at the last moment was replaced by pallid Chautemps and the address on behalf of the absent American Ambassador was delivered by Chargé d'Affaires Murphy. Admiral Long had kindly driven me over, but at table I was placed beside an Oriental journalist who volunteered to present me to *ces dames* of the Opera Ballet troupe. His proposal was of a rare incongruity with Mr. Murphy's excellent though hypnagogic speech on General Washington.

He who drew most applause was General Gouraud, magnificent with his spade beard, grown, he had told Henrietta Ely, to impress the Bedouins with his strength and masculinity. On his breast were the Cross of the Legion of Honor, his Médaille Militaire (bestowed upon the highest generals and the non-commissioned ranks for valor on the field), flanked by a long Croix de Guerre, the colors of the riband obliterated under a bronze of citation palms. He was clad in horizon blue, his uniform bearing five stars on the sleeve.

It was said the magnificent soldier suffered from lapses of memory and he moved uncomfortably on his wounded legs; yet I observed his profile as one which might be struck on a coin. His eyes were serene yet indifferent to that before him, while about him sounded his name as if intoned beneath the dome of the Pantheon, and his hair lay on his brow like a victor's wreath.

A source of entertainment were the movies. Soldiers paid virtually nothing and all patrons were given little maps with their tickets indicating the location of the nearest *abri*. At the beginning of every move, a voice announced that one must keep calm in the event of *alerte*, that all was being done for the patron's safety. Such speeches became as meaningless and disregarded as the colored advertisements flashed upon the screen during the intermissions.

I remember walking along the Champs Elysées during the ululations of the *alerte*. Everywhere on every side the soul-affecting noise came into being, and I saw the faces huddled at the entrance of the *abris*, where the people had been forced to go by the police, looking upward and saying, "Are they ours?" This in May.

Twice I saw planes, but their markings were indistinguishable. One might judge the proximity of the Germans by the sound of the D. C. A. bursts. As each policeman motioned me down, I showed my press card. There was little danger and it was a strange sensation to walk thus through the empty city to the cryings of unseen voices. At either side of the Champs Elysées cars were pulled up by decree, their motors switched off. Occasionally along the great empty lengths of the avenue dashed a staff car at top speed, and occasionally a poison-gas alarm-car passed with its horn sounding like a braying donkey in contrast to the waves from the sirens. It circulated sometimes thus, just for practice, and if one were meticulous, one put on one's gas mask.

In a side street, I remember during such an *alerte* seeing a mad woman walking along and talking in a loud voice to herself as all the concierges and others observed her from their half open doors as she walked past, her voice echoing in the silence preceding the higher note of the "all clear," then suddenly the braying of the gas alarm.

I noted:

"Topical movies are not particularly popular. I refer to two which ran on the Champs Elysées—*An Englishman's Home*, dealing with the activities of a German spy in setting up a radio beam for the purpose of directing enemy aircraft to England, and *The Lion Has Wings*, a saga of British aerial activity, half-boring propaganda. But undoubtedly both of these films have been shown in America. The newsreels are replete with soldiers consuming vast sides of beef with unaffected gusto in the subterranean comfort of the Maginot Line and of Hitler hanging in effigy at a French outpost in reply to German provocation. (The Boches, as they are now unaffectedly called, had hauled an open umbrella to the top of a flagstaff.) On coming out of the movie hall I observed a sign indicating a flight of steps leading downwards and bearing the legend: MIMI PINSON, ABRI DANCING. I've always cherished a nostalgic affection for the lovely grisette who has figured so often in romantic literature, and descended to seek her.

"In the vast, vaulted chamber which bore her name the music was audible as a dull bourdon. I saw countless couples dancing on a crowded floor, their faces pale through drifts of cigarette smoke and quite as expressionless as gas masks. I shuddered mildly as I turned to wander up the shrouded Champs Elysées, guided by the flickering of the flame under the Arc. In the blackout it has assumed a strange brilliancy."

With Jean and Adrian and, I believe, Hankey, we made an excursion to the rue de Lapp. We ventured down the black narrow street with its red lanterns muffled as were more decent lights. Its doors occasionally swinging open to give us glimpses of pink flesh and snatches of noise, we entered an establishment.

The place was filled with Sénégalese and their tattooed faces beaming beneath their fez, drunken white soldiers and assorted civilians. We sat at a table and soon the patronne came over and talked with us. A fine-looking woman she was and she handled the men magnificently, slapping them and sending them on their way if they dawdled too long, and collecting her fee of ten francs with great efficiency yet without apparent system. The women, stark naked, were like placid cows, young and buxom and not unpretty. I looked at the women, the Senegalese, the drunken soldiery, and saw it as bestiality, without subterfuge, without yearning or a twisting of the wits.

"What wonderful German propaganda this would be," interjected one of my companions, and there is no doubt he was correct, but somehow it was natural like a farmyard, having less function, but being not more degenerate than state-approved sensuality in Germany.

"What do they do when the *alerte* goes?" I asked.

"Oh, they all go down in the cellars."

"Even in the better bordellos?" I insisted, "It must be very embarrassing to the uniformless officers to be packed thus together… rather *folichon*."

"C'est la guerre."

The next day, I saw Mr. Kemp and Morty Singer who were very active in their various *oeuvre*s, particularly the American Aid where one might see American Volunteer Ambulance Service men and citizens wishing repatriation, and various members of the American Red Cross such as Maloney and Pamp acting in France under

Messrs. Swift, Chatfield-Taylor, Carter and others. Morty introduced me to the admirable freelance photographer, Miss Thérèse Bonney. Twice decorated, she had but recently returned from Switzerland and was active in the compilation of a photographic history of the war which, I believe, has become an official Congressional document.

About this time I first heard of Ted Schulze's unit. Apparently he had been at a university in the West when he suddenly became disgusted with it, threw his bag in a car, purchased ten Chevrolet ambulances and with them arrived in France to present his services to the Polish Army.

Silent and well over six feet tall, he was only twenty-one years old.

I had met him in Switzerland two years before when he was on his holidays from Cambridge, and I arranged an interview between Mr. Kemp, Mr. Singer, and Schulze in an attempt to persuade the latter to join forces with us in our Ambulance Corps since we considered it bad policy to have two separate volunteer ambulance sections operating in the field with one Polish division. Schulze was, however, very wary since, as the result of a misunderstanding, he associated Mr. Kemp with a gentleman who had criticized his ability, and we never did unite our organization, the units of which were due to arrive at any moment with his which he had named PAVAS, or Polish American Volunteer Ambulance Service.

I remember walking around to Roger Bérard's apartment near the Ecole Militaire, a quarter of Paris newly built over with seven-storied, ugly, yet not charmless apartment buildings, to make an attempt at talking Ted over. But he was of a very firm disposition and reticent with an Anglo-Saxon stubbornness I found difficult, and refused to change his stand. Bérard was training to be an officer and was magnificent in boots and sky blue kepi. Both posed on the balcony with the Medal of Merit Schulze had received the same morning from General Sikorski on the occasion of the official presentation to be photographed by Madame Bérard. During this operation, I looked about me at the apartment furnished with much rococo and modern equivalents, a strange profusion of bric-a-brac among which I discerned a Negro carved from wood and painted in yellow robes standing non-functionally in a dining room, undersized, yet airy with Spring.

Schulze had recruited various Americans in Paris to drive and they were sent to that camp, which I had the privilege of inspecting two months before, in order to train. Much to Schulze's disgust, they were made to perform most errands for the division since but few of the Poles could drive.

Soon there was activity in the air of one sort or another. People were no longer waiting. With the approach of the *Saison Mondaine*, ladies were flocking to town, quite bored with enforced rustication in draughty châteaux, to see the sights and new collections as well as to get a permanent wave.

Maxim's, at which I had once dined alone, was filled and all the panache of Paris was at its gayest before the cisterns should run dry, the champagne flowed down uncaring gullets, the models paraded at Creed's and Chanel and Maggy Rouff and to this latter place I went at the invitation of the Princesse de Caraman-Chimay and saw a preview of the fashionable stripes French women should wear the coming summer.

The theatres were overflowing. It was a gala season. I left for the country for the last time, for a week or two of respite to conclude my war-born novel, which I had hoped to finish in time for the *Atlantic* novel competition, to close the Abbaye and say goodbye since I had decided to serve in the Polish ambulance corps before returning home. In anticipation of my service I had ordered a uniform at Creed's so magnificent that "in the shade with the light behind me" I might be taken for a general, and boots at Lobb, and Schulze later urged me to buy a Sam Browne belt which I did at Hermes', vowing to myself that, should I be killed, my grave clothes should at least be of quality despite visions of covetous, pleased, hand-rubbing tailors, and my own empty coffers.

WAR: ALLEGRO

DEAREST MOTHER AND FATHER:

I'm in the country once again, and the place looks wonderfully well—today I felt the sun quite hot, and Jeanne's husband is *en permission agricole* which is very convenient, for he is free to help Philippe.

The weather shifts continually from sun to rain, and the sea occasionally pounds the *falaise* quite audibly, but for the most part is quiet enough.

Philippe has got after the garden, and I must admit it looks productive; the walks *ratissées* and the new éspaliers bound with reeds to wires running between stakes set at the corners of the plots. The green house is full of energetically sprouting plants, the birds sing and Spring is much in evidence, with all the subtle yearnings and stretchings.

Philippe has planted four more cypresses, two at either side of the ones flanking the grill leading into the vegetable gardens. It looks very well.

Of our neighbors, an acquaintance occupied himself, until called for military service, with teaching English in a village school. He admitted later that, after such an experience, trench warfare might hold but little terror. Several girls of the vicinity have made a wartime work of teaching, preferring it to knitting interminable sweaters.

Women whose husbands are mobilized tend to the heavy work in the running of their châteaux and farms. Such a one as the latter, I followed at a distance down the village road. Arrayed in a rusty black coat, faded green dress and sabots, her hair escaping from a ragged cloth wound about her head, she labored at carrying an overflowing zinc water-sprinkler to her little garden. With the swaying of her thin shoulders, puddles fell to the ground, and I became conscious of the pathetico-admirable, inefficient determinedness of these deserted women surrounded by broods of children in whose upturned faces they may at times, and with a sigh of course, trace the lineaments of some far-away Barbu.

And I noted in the changing light of nascent Spring and impending death that: "In the country, the war makes itself evident in intimations of which I received two this afternoon in walking through the village and on the cliffs.

"Under the great lime tree which shades 'l'Auberge du Soleil Levant; Garnaveau, Prop.' was heaped an assortment of wheel-rims, milk containers which had lost their coating of zinc, stoves, and the usual collection of rusted oddments which are forever lying in the inconspicuous corners of farms. Just above, as if to explain their presence was the familiar tricolor poster which reminds one, above a serried rank of printed bayonets, that 'it is of steel that victories are forged.' If each village of two hundred inhabitants produces such a quantity of potential weapons there exists little danger of the factories running short of materials, yet more significant perhaps is the fact that the frugal French are playing a game at which they cannot be beat, that of improvisation and economy.

"Yet a week later, I was to note sadly that the *Garde Champêtre*, the aged village policeman, to the beating of his drum, proclaimed in the intersection of roads which passed for the village square that a fine would be applied to those who continued to steal from the pile of piteous scrap metal.

"The cliffs were quite deserted save for my friend David who sat on a flat rock looking out to sea in the direction of the fishing fleet from Port-en-Bessin tacking toward the Cotentin. We had a word, and I continued on in the cold, over the great pebbles which constitute the beach. It seems incredible that tomorrow will be May.

"The noise of the sea filled my ears, yet some unidentified instinct constrained me to look upward, and I saw above me a biplane, its motors barely turning the propellors, flying at what appeared to me an incredibly low altitude. Like a soaring gull it passed beyond the cliffs.

"On my return, David told me that it was of the coast patrol. He seemed well informed on the subject, adding that the planes used were old ships remarkable for their ability to remain aloft at relatively slow speeds, thus facilitating observation. He added that he saw them pass every day, and that once they threw him cigarettes.

"A week or two ago a Naval aquaplane landed near the cliffs for an unknown reason. The sea washed it against the rocks, and one pontoon having received some slight damage, it was decided she could not take off. Great trucks came to Longues to the delight of the village girls, for sailors came to take the plane to pieces, then drove off with it to an unknown destination.

"The next morning, the village girls, arrayed in their best, called at all the houses to sell tricolor cockades on which was printed *Secours National.* Undertaken on a nationwide basis, the collection netted $500,000 for the benefit of 'Veuves de guerre'; war widows already.

"I was told that three young soldiers of the region had met their deaths 'for the glory of France on the field of Honor.' One, from Bayeux, left an aged mother and father. The latter was a *grand mutilé*, a 'great mutilated,' of the last war.

"His mother was pointed out to me by my Spanish grocer as I sought to buy olive oil. There is none to be had. Sugar is to be rationed next month, and ordinary soap is difficult to procure while one is allowed but fifty kilos of coal a month. As a result, in the country, as in the city, one is constrained to take but few baths. But there are many concessions in rustication; days of sun, hash made from the remnants of Sunday meat on city's meatless Mondays, apple blossoms, and the pleasant conviction that things are surely much, much worse in Germany.

"The wall has fallen down and I went in to Bayeux to see the architect, for if I make arrangements for masons *now* the wall might be up by Summer.

"I sat in his pleasant quiet study, and complimented him on the burgeoning garden beyond the parted windows, and on the beauty of the pear blossoms enameling the espaliers. Above and beyond his walls rose the duplicate spires of Bayeux Cathedral; the tiles were wet with a recent flurry of rain. The air was electric with storm and the vanes pointed Northeast 'Oui,' he smiled, 'tout indique la guerre.'...

"Yesterday I had a Porto with the Commandant de G. who had been summoned from retirement to become a member of a commission to purchase horses in Kansas City and was but just returned. This admirable man, who has but one arm, yet manages to shoot over his spaniel and drive his own car, spoke of the delightful reception he'd been given in America and was proud of the fact that but three per cent of his charges, rather than eighteen per cent as in the last great war, died en route.

"'But, one was killed and the conditions of its death were such as not to preclude the possibility of sabotage,' he stated with a suspicious look in the direction of the door, a prerogative of the discussion of official military business. He downed his port and curled his mustache, adopting a firm and reminiscent expression, not unmixed with the satisfaction of duty well done. Poor fellow.

"I find reserve officers of a certain age not displeased with their part in the war for there is always joy in the reassumption of authority one had believed forever abdicated. Yet such pleasure must be short-lived when confronted with sons in uniform....

"Norman fields are bordered by hillocks, most probably the moss-grown remnants of fallen walls. In crossing such a one, I came upon a small boy seated in a furrow of the noon-deserted field. He was engaged in the making of a sling shot, patent excuse for conversation.

"It appeared he was a refugee from Paris where he left his mother teaching in an advanced school. He had come to the country with a small pig-tailed sister (Mademoiselle Poupette) to whom, on evincing the desire, I was formally presented. She was a charming girl with a pink dress and blue apron the color of her china eyes. The children lived with their grandmother.

"To my amazement I later discovered Mademoiselle Poupette was the natural child of a gentleman I have mentioned in these pages as meeting in Paris. 'C'est du Balzac,' exclaimed Cabestan on our stumbling on the truth together.

"With the superiority of the Parisian born and bred, the boy said that though he was bored in the country, he managed to amuse himself with climbing on the steep *falaise*, nesting for crows' eggs (etiquette forbade me to evince any doubt of his having accomplished this well-nigh impossible feat), in building huts and the like, especially astonishing his peasant contemporaries. To me, a brother city-dweller, he confessed interest in the tender wheat shoots, in the reptilean necks of the asparagus coiling from their patches of sandy earth.

"From his conversation I assumed, to be later proved correct, that advanced education is carried on in the larger centers alone; that the villages have elementary schools, the teachers delegated to these last being more or less make-shift. The arrangement is consummately excellent, for the older children are quite able to pedal a few kilometers to the local center and there, despite huge classes, benefit from the instruction of adequately qualified professors, while for the younger ones who cannot go far from home, the make-shift education is quite sufficient.

"On walking home on the new grass at the side of the road in the twilight and gray-green austerity of the village, I overtook Monsieur David, who lived on his pension as *ancien chef de gare* in a small trellised house near the church of Longues. He carried a rake and spade over his shoulder, and his face assumed lines of reminiscent grief for he told me he had but come away from seeding his wife's grave, as was custom the eve of Palm Sunday.

"About his neck he wore a shining yellow collar, which I suspected as being of celluloid, and a great copper collar button gleamed and bobbed with his words, and he measured his periods by stopping and blowing his nose in a vast crimson cloth which might have seen service as his station-master's flag.

"David is a great shrimp fisherman, and spends most of the season among the algae and rocks at the foot of the cliffs in search of that elusive crustacea. 'The largest some times the length of my middle finger!' he would invariably announce when discussing his prowess. There was a pleasant element of sportsman's pride in his nature, and he would sometimes present me with a mess of his wriggling catch which proved excellent eating. In the same spirit, the Curé would send me a pot of his honey, which he gleaned at the cost of stings on his fat hands, from the angry bourdon of his hives, and I return the compliment with a bottle of Calvados 'as old as the gardener's grandmother' distilled from apples prepared on the Abbaye's ancient press. The bottle was smuggled by David or the Curé under coat or cassock to avoid paying the tax due the Government if one's fermentation were taken from one's land. But now I no longer saw David as going proudly from under the gate in the twilight, his crayfish net obliquely over his shoulder, but rather alone and coatless in the grave yard. He turns the new earth of his wife's grave to the melancholy trickling of the fountain beneath its warning of *Eau non potable*, perhaps observed by the cat slowly blinking its striated eyes, to the rays of a dying sun and the scent of the human earth.

"Walking beside him in the twilight I smelt the smoke blown low from the chimney pots and heard swallows twitter as they flew from under the eaves, and the banging of closing shutters, and the ding-dong of Vespers rung to the rheumatic cadence of the Curé's aged arms, and I listened to David's cider-roughened voice as he spoke of this war and the last and what he termed the 'good days before.'

"I often think it a strange habit, that which men have of attempting to evoke the spirit of an era by reference to its effervescence, to the material things which it produced; as well evoke the sea by the débris which it casts up on the shore.

"Poor David spoke of d'Aumonts and four-in-hands driven four abreast, 'by cockaded coachmen on the Avenue de l'Imperatrice, the hubs of their whirring yellow wheels but a few finger breadths part, with a man at the rear who played on a trumpet the while' as if the carriages and luxury of his youth were responsible for what in retrospect he considers the stability and calm of that era.

"He was plainly no longer pleased with life and shook his realistic Norman head at what he deemed the immorality of the village. The lack of idealism—had he not caught lovers amongst the graves?—and the war. Yet the latter did not affect him materially, as a retired civil-servant, a station-master in fact, of the Government railroads, he was too old for mobilization and benefited fully from his pension; yet he experienced the pressures of hidden hands which hurried him at dinner, and made him less agile at catching crayfish. 'Is it that I can't enjoy myself when the world is in pain?' he stopped and asked me. His eyes were opaque in tears."

So life continued untroubled before the ululations, the wild crescendo, the deafening eruptions from the East. Philippe stuffed everything that came to his hand into the furnace to heat the water for my bath, asparagus bits from my luncheon, the entrails of the guinea hens I ate to save the grain, and in waiting I noted pointless minutiae in my Journal, war trivia indeed, my subconscious perhaps giving ear to coming events, my attention but half given to a story but half told, my eyes on the straws in the wind....

"It is warmer this afternoon and the cock or weather vane on the refectory has swung around and the wind is from the right direction. Philippe says we'll be spared cold but suffer rain. On my walk by the cliffs I saw an object floating. It was alive but not a bird for it disappeared for minutes at a time beneath the surface, a monster perhaps, or as Father might say a 'live mine.'

"I saw Madame Métais, the antique dealer at Bayeux, and she informed me that her roof mender had been installing tiles on barracks dedicated to the use, or future use, of Communists who are to be sent out shortly from Paris. I'm sure they'll be subject of numerous atrocity stories *in re* concentration camps, etc. It is rather extraordinary how the woman, so intelligent and clever in what concerns her, *pataugeait*, floated, in matters of essential national policy—it was as if they did not affect her as irrevocably as whether or no the roof mender got around to repairing her roof rather than working on the camp.

"I have purchased tickets, ten in number, in the National Lottery. I was prepared to win the 5,000,000 francs and was complimenting myself on the wise way I should administer the spending of my wealth when Jeanne (after a perusal of the newspapers) informed me I had won thirty-five francs.

"She also tells me the black cat I found miawing pathetically on the *falaise* has killed an immense rat and entered with same in its mouth with proud and triumphant air in the kitchen. Rats are everywhere—I shall spread poisoned grain to tempt the greedy rodents to their deaths. All about me, over the ceiling, in the walls range the rodents, their hairless feet padding between the dropping of the rain.

"This morning I discovered a dead cock and it transpired from Jeanne that the weird moping which disturbed me last night might well be ascribed to an owl, which sensing death, gave vent to eery emotions—what a basis for superstition—evidently the same hooting was heard on the death of a rabbit..."

Bored with inactivity where I felt much was intimated, I decided to have a dinner and asked all the neighbors; the Douville, the Duchesse d'Harcourt, whose latest book it was planned I should translate, Daisy de Broglie, her father, the Marquis de Balleroy, Isabelle Foy and her mother Comtesse Foy, Colibris de la Barre-de-Nanteuil and others as well as Georges Perrin of the Swiss Foreign Office, Hankey and Cabestan. The last three I hoped would discuss the then stagnant international situation from their various points of view and vantage. My two turkeys, dubbed "Hitler" and "Stalin" by the Longs, since they were unsympathetic to their barnyard companions, I ordered to be executed and went in town to engage a refugee chef of note who, it was rumored, had taken up residence at Bayeux. I also passed the Estaminet and purchased a bottle of "Johnnie Valkère" from the giggling barmaid.

In our woods filled with jonquils and Spanish refugees gleaning dead twigs, I felled a dead tree, not without surly looks from the interlopers. It was stuffed into our stove, the concentric iron rings of which glowed in appreciation. Jeanne forgot the dignity of maternity and under the terrifying scowl of Savarin cleaned the turkeys and pots and shelled the new peas and cut the hearts from the artichokes, while I with my great keys entered the mildewed regions of the cellar to the dismay of scuttling spiders and lifted the dust covered wines from the bins.

The table was set and the great birds rotated majestically before the flames, the still air was heavy with odors from the gardens, the decanting, and the steams from the pots and pans.

My three diplomatic friends were to arrive on the Cherbourg Express and I backed out the Commerciale preparatory to driving down to the station. No sooner had the motor fired than I heard the ringing of the telephone. A telegram from Hankey: "So sorry I cannot come," and then the ringing again and yet another from Cabestan with much the same message. I waited for a third, yet silence; and I went to the station and saw Georges' sharp searching face among the crowds and then its sudden relaxation in a smile of recognition.

"Ah mon ami, at least *you've* come!"

"Yes, I was in Paris and might have gone back but what's the use, Switzerland is not at war though Holland and Belgium have but just been raped."

As we heard his words confirmed an hour later over the radio, the opening bars of the *Marseillaise* which prefaced every official broadcast were the earnest of a tragic voice. Later when the broadcasting became impaired the strangling notes were the dying voice of France.

The telephone rang again; the Guichard could not come, Doudouce must be transported and immediately to be midwifed in the Clinic at Bayeux—result a girl, Isabelle, in one hour and a half. And Isabelle Foy took no cocktail and soon drove off with Daisy de Broglie, the Duchesse and the Marquis.

The next morning Isabelle Foy telephoned to say that she had been "requisitioned" by the sub-prefect to meet the children of the King of Belgium with their entourage of maids and valets and tutors, that the reception had been in secret.

Near the Foy château of Etreham, a Monsieur Olivier had purchased a little house some five years before. Monsieur Olivier had never put in an appearance yet the house was always well kept though no one knew what passed behind the drawn blinds. The royal children went directly to this house for "Monsieur Olivier" was their father.

Near the Douville-Maillefeu's place at Bernières was a château which had been devised to Hitler. At the time it had been considered a huge joke and the deceased exproprietor a bit mad. Now I suppose the villagers are laughing out of the other side of their mouth.

Yet soon the royal caravan passed on and into Spain and at one time crowd-born rumors circulated to the effect that the royal children should be kept as hostages in revenge for their father's perfidy.

And soon there were more witnesses of flight from Belgium. Cars riddled with bullets, their roofs covered with mattresses as make-shift protection against bomb splinters, came into our green Normandy with haggard men at the wheel and mothers with dead babies in their arms. Such a one I saw arrive at Bayeux, the crowds silent with rage as a child was taken from a woman's arms; as for her, she lay back, the evocation of a cry for help on the blood spattered seat of the little town car with its unfamiliar red and white license plates.

It was the September evacuations all over again and yet this time it was not a picnic as I went with Daisy to various stores to requisition furniture and plates and forks and stoves to outfit a canteen at the Bayeux station. On every side one heard the same refrain, "Oh les pauvres," and to Longues came eleven of the Guichard's Belgian cousins. A fellow of twenty-nine who was not mobilized, since he was the father of three children, told me he had driven from Maastricht, that he had stopped by the side of the road to sleep and in the night, hearing strange noises, looked over the side and saw German tanks lumbering by in the darkness close at either hand. "It was like having a whale come up beside one in a rowboat; one could but hold one's breath and hope one's heart would not burst." At the sub-prefect's office, where I had gone to offer him on behalf of my parents a hotel to be used as a children's hospital, I saw two young Belgians who wished to be repatriated so that they might fight.

"Haven't you been mobilized?" said the sub-prefect.

"No, sir, our class has not been called and we wish to volunteer."

They were in their twenties. Everywhere on the crowded roads were more tragic examples of lack of preparedness in Belgium; the baggage lashed to the rear of the cars, baby carriages, sewing machines, and golf clubs were evidence of the distraction which seized these people, of the urgency in which they lost their wits. On every side one heard stories which from their novelty brought tears and cries to the eyes and throat—the war had been so far away and now it was so near....A man had forgotten something in his house. He left his wife and children in the car. On his return, he saw his son slump crookedly with a little gasp. A spent machine-gun bullet had passed through his neck. The child he buried immediately in his garden. A woman left Ghent with seven children and arrived at Bayeux with two.

As one considers from a distance one concludes they were fools to run, but I suppose France seemed so safe and they were ill-prepared for calamity and had run when it came. But for the most part they did not realize what had happened and walked about in a dazed fashion which made things all the more difficult, or acted as if nothing had happened which was not sane but grotesque. Normandy was so peaceful they could not believe what they had fled before.

Daisy and the Duchesse d'Harcourt came to the Abbaye and it was decided I should go to Paris to see Mr. Chatfield-Taylor in an attempt to have more money apportioned to Normandy from the funds of the American Red Cross. I shut the *Maison Abbatiale*, the shutters and the cupboard doors, walked once more in the nascent gardens and through the *potager* and listened to the philosophic tinkling of the source and left once sweet Normandy for good. I left for Paris.

I did not find Mr. Chatfield-Taylor but Daisy having come down, we drove to Morgan and Company and I presented her to Mr. Bernard Carter who was of the Red Cross Committee. He explained the situation with clarity; that the American Red Cross in giving money to the French could but advise what should be done with it having no jurisdiction over the funds once given. Daisy threw her hands in the air and we all three knew she would get nothing since the French Red Cross was trammeled with red-tape and politics.

Mr. Carter said he would speak of the situation in Normandy. Yes, he would repeat that in the North every available spot was filled with the three successive waves of refugees; the Spanish Communists of the Spanish Civil War, the French and now the Belgians.

Having done what we could, we retreated.

I saw Robert Montgomery. He was very much in a rush to get his uniform to leave with the American Field Service but nonetheless agreed to see me the next afternoon at the Travelers' Club. While waiting for him to turn up, I saw a British officer of my acquaintance, an elderly gentleman of great kindness, who said he had just received word that his nephew and sole heir had been wounded at Dunkirk and was about to die.

"I don't know what to do. We've had the title since the twelfth century and now this is the end. Perhaps one of my American cousins would be willing to carry on."

And Montgomery and the English gentleman and I had a drink and spoke as was habit of the last months, of nothing. Soon the war would give a coherency which could be understood and appreciated in all its frightening implications. But now events moved too rapidly and later we would be dulled with calamity.

Montgomery's briefish career in the Ambulance Corps was not in the least cut short by his own wish. His brother drivers whom I saw later were determined to ignore him did they find him the least bit Hollywoodish, but after the first day they discovered he was a very good fellow and were sorry to see him go.

Apparently his contract did not permit him to take risks and, on applying to a member of the corps who was a lawyer to get him out of contractual difficulties, the lawyer is said to have answered:

"We don't care whether you stay or leave now that you've given the Field Service the publicity we want," which was rather abrupt and certainly turned the tables on Hollywood.

Over at the American Aid, neither Morty Singer nor Mr. Kemp had news of the arrival of the Polish ambulances. Since Schulze had earlier invited me, I decided rather than to wait for ours to leave with his group which was to move up to the Front in a week or so to study their liaison with the Polish Army.

Usually autonomous or self-directed were the volunteer

ambulance sections with a liaison officer of the regular Army to give advice and to transmit commands. The latter's job; particularly in the case of Count Antoni Wielopolski, Schulze's liaison officer, was a difficult one and had to be handled with great tact for Schulze who had started as a sergeant, was by June a two-star lieutenant and Wielopolski's superior officer. Also he was dissatisfied with his lot since he had been left at the base camp to do the errands and be shown off to visiting notables since the day of his arrival. The men were all grumbling and threatening to quit unless they were sent on active service, and Schulze intimated that he might go over to the French since he considered he might there be more useful. Since he was head-strong and his stepfather the American Ambassador, poor Wielopolski shuddered.

To get my military papers, I went to the Franco-Polish Mission and asked the guard if I might see General Denain. No, the General was not in but if I would wait, his *chef de cabinet*, President Pierre Cathala might be able to fit me into his schedule of appointments.

Captain Cathala very kindly gave me what I wished and said the General was away since he had but just learned his château was burned to the ground. A week before he had lost his two sons in the aviation.

On the way over to the Regina to start the ball rolling on my Polish military papers which were a bit special (I did not wish to sign up for six months, but merely a pass to last while I studied the liaison until our ambulances should arrive), I was stopped twice to have my papers examined, the cab being whistled over to the curb for the purpose. "It's because of Mandel," explained the taxi driver deprecatingly. Later my papers were to be examined seven times in one day. To test the efficiency of the examiners I showed a different document at each examination: my passport, my press card, my *laissez passer*, my *permis de circuler*, the paper I had just received from Cathala, and my driver's license. Perhaps it was since each of these documents stated I was American that I was not troubled more than I was, yet it was evident to me that in half of the cases the officers were not in a position to judge the authenticity of that which they examined. Certainly in the night clubs where they often penetrated they could not make out the writing on the miserable little identity cards. Often at noon, they would form a cordon about the cafés examining the papers of everyone present in zealous inefficiency.

With Goekoop I visited the apartments of several women whom he judged suspect. Two in particular excited his attention, and yet the French did nothing though he had pointed them out to my friends of the Ministry of the Interior who felt themselves incapable of action, as in the case of Baronne Z., because the women's papers were "in order" as are the passports of half the crew of the *S.S. Manhattan*. The women occupied an apartment on the top floor of a modern building near the Invalides equipped with a private elevator and standing beside a hotel which, as in the case of the Continental, had been transformed into a Ministry. They had not bothered to furnish more than the two rooms of the ten-room apartment for which the concierge informed us the rental paid was 30,000 francs a year unfurnished. That the other eight rooms stood vacant I observed as I walked about the quadrilateral terrace which commanded a magnificent view of the center of Paris.

"What a spot for signaling! It commands all Paris..."

In driving to Jacqueline de Broglie's who chose to live in a little apartment on the Left Bank rather than out in Neuilly with her mother, Mrs. Reginald Fellowes, we passed huge street-cleaning trucks parked along the center of the Champs Elysées. We stopped to ask what they were for. The policeman refused to answer till he noticed the yellow diplomatic license plates then said, "So planes won't land on the avenue at night. It's come to that." Then as if he had said too much, he hunched the sling of his rifle higher on his shoulder and turned away.

That night I went to the Gare du Nord at Jacqueline's invitation to see the trains come in from Belgium. Jacqueline was dressed in a tan uniform of a Femme de France. Under the blue-lighted, noisy, girdered vault of the station, she went about doing her work with the boy scouts, military stretcher bearers and porters. One train after another arrived through the night, laden with refugees. The old men and women were the most talkative for in situations of real stress they are the most adventuresome; their refrain was the same, "We have left everything, but everything..."

Operating room and delivery rooms were adjacent to the tracks; as I passed, the door swung open and I saw two bloody feet protruding over the edge of a first-aid dressing table. By the door were stacked rows of blood-drenched stretchers. The Nazi attack consisted in sawing off the tops of the railroad carriages with machine-gun fire and then they made mincemeat of those packed within. Thus occasionally when the trains arrived shrieks arose above the escaping steam of the engines.

Everywhere people slept on their bundles and one old man was cursing the Government for having made him pay for his ticket on the train. Jacqueline shouted at me in English for a hundred francs and gave it to the man saying it was from the Republic with its compliments.

Tea and coffee and bread were given them, the bread covered with honey for the children to supply them with extra vitamins before packing them into Paris auto-buses and sending them to barracks vacated by regiments entering the Line, or into the buildings left empty by evacuees from Paris.

I wrote of all this and gave the articles to Pamp and Maloney of the Red Cross, neither of whom spoke any French. It was a miracle they got work done. Miss Ely was particularly shocked that the American Red Cross should send over men who understood the French so little. Later in Bordeaux, when her great friend, General Gouraud, came into a restaurant looking like a St. George with a broken wing, it was inconceivable to her that they had never heard of him and could not understand the implication of tragedy in the eyes of the one-time Governor of Paris, he who had ordered his arm amputated to hasten a too-lengthy convalescence. It is with triviality that most men's hearts are touched for the heart is trivial, and the ability to appreciate triviality lies in intimate and sympathetic knowledge; yet to help a people in catastrophe I suppose it is not necessary to understand their culture.

I gave up my apartment and said goodbye to brave Fanny my maid, and took a room at the Club. At Morgan's I made arrangements to have my things shipped from Paris and gave them one of my manuscripts which Miss Harle had just completed. The other I gave to Helen Rodgers of the American Embassy who was kind enough to take it down to Bordeaux with her. In common with others I was preoccupied that my work should not perish.

And then I went once again to battle with the bureaucracy at the Regina—always they would pass me on to someone else who would be out until I got into a state of fictitious desperation and then at last things turned for the better and I received my papers. My position was unique since I had the rank of Aspirant Lieutenant, a commission terminable at my own will in the Polish Army, the while continuing on as a journalist.

Next I went and purchased a sleeping bag and a musette at Vuitton's and in it stuffed three khaki shirts, three pairs of socks, a box of 100 Sobrani cigarettes—the last and best in Paris for dying men—a tooth brush and soap and that was all with my Journal and a copy of *Werther* (I bought it at the Uniprix, the French equivalent of Woolworth's for two francs, all I cared to spend for the intellectual impartiality implied by Goethe), another of *Alice in Wonderland* and Birkenhead's *Selection of English Letters*, with a sweater and a trench coat over my arm. And then I went for a walk in Paris.

Schulze was at his stepfather's hôtel in the rue des Saints-Pères. There I found him with two bearded drivers and he told me to meet him at the Meurice at five when he should have definite orders. But of one thing he was certain, that we should leave Paris for the Front that night.

It was three in the afternoon and the sky was of a strange murkiness and veiled, yet streaked red from the sun.

The days were to be of chaos, of unfinished meals and bloodiness, of lurid horizons and spilled champagne, of musty death and concussion, of fatigue and interrupted sleep.

The next day, a Monday, the 10th of June, my back against an elm shading the château of Corbéville near Orsay, a village to the South of Paris, I sat with my journal on my knees writing of the preceding day, of the manner in which we had left Paris to join the First Tank Brigade of the Polish Army in France bivouacked in the woods. And today I read on the dirty page:

"Sunday, June 9th—Out to Le Vezidon with Schulze, our Lieutenant to get Graaf, our second-in-command. One is an American, the other Swiss I force myself to think. I heard my first bombs strike at either side with sounds much as paper bags exploding. I saw an object in the sky and stopped on thinking it a parachute, but on further inspection it proved to be merely shrapnel smoke undissolved in the windless heavy air. Paris had an atmosphere of awful static; a car flamed unattended in the middle of the Champs Elysées, pitted for as yet uninstalled anti-plane landing posts. The big trucks stationed at the center of the avenue have been used in the evacuation, a car wrecked in the morning had not been removed—this by the Opera. Near the Etoile we passed young girls in shorts riding tandems, the luggage carriers of their bicycles were laden with flowers they had brought in from the country. Everywhere stand groups sensing danger. Events are of such rapidity that the population has not time to readjust itself to actual and impending horror.

"Graaf's place proved to be a *fin-de-siècle* white pavilion at which we were received by anonymous people who offered us tea; we went with anonymous but friendly children to feed their rabbits in the farm. It is fortunate the young lack understanding since its absence lends an effect of consummate philosophy in keeping them calm. I was glad to be in khaki among these civilians. A uniform is armor against hysteria. I am accepted as the man I show myself to be. People have no time for complicated judgments. In the emotional simplicity of great exhilaration, I am accepted because I am an officer in the allied forces.

"Soon we returned again to Paris to leave at eight in the strange oppressive light of gray clouds through which came fitful rays of a dying sun over the city, like the grayness of smoke through which one may see lurid tongues of flame. Panic was in the air and civilian traffic was fast and seemingly jerky and the cars badly driven. We drove slowly and dinnerless, and I helmetless since none was issued me, and we did not know where. Soon we plunged in utter darkness, dislocating an axle from the spring on one of the cars as the result of a collision, and it was abandoned by the side of the road.

"We arrived at Orsay, Southwest of Paris at 11:15 P.M. That the village was Orsay was kept from us, a stupid regulation since three of our cars, lost in the darkness were to have great difficulty in finding us since they did not know to what spot they should drive.

"The brigade is everywhere in the woods and I lay at the foot of a tree stretched out on the ground in my un-water-proofed sleeping-bag—this after identity papers were checked in the gloom of the château by a non-committal non-commissioned officer. Sleep was impossible since the night was made hideous with the exhausts of small gasoline motors recharging depleted batteries, of lampless motorcycles driven through the woods and later the roar of bombers and the patter in the woods of our descending anti-aircraft shrapnel. I remembered a man whom I had seen hit with such shrapnel; striking him in the neck the jagged pellet was found in his trousers. I rather envied the German aviators so high and clean and well-fed above for we were given nothing; as I leaned against the trunk of the tree with death pattering in the leaves about me, I watched the livid fingers of the search lights."

On arriving at Orsay, the Traitor of Stuttgaart had announced the position of the Black Brigade on the radio. We were so named in derogation of threatened vengeance by the Germans since the First Tank Brigade under the Command of General Matchek, had been among troops to advance effectively, though in vain, against Nazi lightning in Poland. Resistance was resented. The Traitor, six hundred kilometers away, knew the Black Brigade lay in the woods of Orsay twenty-four hours after the tanks had arrived, though we of the ambulance section had not known to what front we were driving.

As I heard the shells whistling over Orsay I felt an absurd fondness for my Chevrolet ambulance, I thought with a smile that such emotion might be excusable were it expended on a Spitfire or Hurricane.

The château of Corbéville in the style of Henri IV, small, turreted and of red brick, is situated high on the foliaged hill above Orsay. It was here we breakfasted with the officers of the First Tank Brigade, I admired the dismantled chamber in which we sat at table with its tall windows and gray paneling; I wondered to whom the château might have belonged. The while an orderly, quite as much of an anachronism as the scene about me with his pitiable military self-conscious effacement and cropped hair, poured coffee into a large china bowl on the table before me. It is all too rapid; I must still smile at such evidences of militarism. Through the steam I saw the officers with a strange humor of cynicism yet affection.

Before breakfast I had followed a path leading down the hill and in the wet fields I passed men squatting prey to the anachronism of shame since they hid their faces in their caps at my approach and then young girls in the fields. The girls were sunburned and smiling, and offered me some strawberries.

"Merci bien, mesdemoiselles!" The strawberries were very good. How kind and pretty were the girls, and how brave one feels as one salutes!

The roads near Orsay were filled with refugees from Paris and on the cars were lashed mattresses as I had seen them earlier on the roads from Belgium.

All day the Polish soldiers practiced on their motorcycles (there had been but six thousand automobiles in Poland and a vast majority of recruits lacked mechanical knowledge), the small machines reminding me of overladen beasts; or the men stood under their field showers washing unpierced bodies, their skin white in contrast with their sunburned faces and arms, and gold chains with medallions of Saints about their necks. I watched and shrugged and waited for the evening when we must leave.

Yet that afternoon I experienced a strange chiaroscuro—a strange contrast in War and Peace. A staff lieutenant was to drive to Paris and I made arrangements to return with him to Metropolis. I was quite certain that Paris should fail. With the Army it was evident from the General who paced alone in his garden to the birds which were deserting Orsay and flying South.... If one put one's ear to the ground it was as if one heard the rumble of the tanks and the air about one eddied to the distant, inaudible sound of fire. One's unsolicited perceptions taunted one with the truth.

He was a pleasant companion, the lieutenant, and the chauffeur drove at great speed against the uneven tide from Paris. Once we were stopped and our papers examined.

"But Lieutenant, that is not a seven but a four," protested the policeman pointing with his big finger, his head stuck through the lowered window of the car. "The pass is issued not for a week but for four days only, and this is the fifth day."

The Lieutenant turned to me.

"The man is mad. I made the pass out myself; I shall make myself another good for thirty days." And so saying, he did. Many officers had such blanks. The policeman waved us on. Along the crowded roads the new rifle lashed to the side leaped in its raw straps, the gas masks banged together as we careened over the road from curb to curb.

Arrived in Paris, we found it in a strange state of alarm, yet individuals at Morgan's Bank still believed, this the eleventh day of June, that Paris could not fall, and to my friend, Monsieur Lasalle of the Postal Department, I felt I must be circumspect in giving my reasons for hastening my effects out of Paris. I'd often spoken with him about his son who was in the Chasseurs Alpins, and I had a great respect for Lasalle and the indignation which made him wild as the Frenchmen of the last war were wild, wild with indignation at what they would not understand and could not tolerate. The streets were virtually emptied, yet many shops were still open and I walked slowly across the Place Vendôme to the car.

Later it was the one vehicle parked on the empty length of the Champs Elysées, and we the only ones in the Club, there to drink a bottle of champagne, to hear the bells of the city and the occasional firing of the anti-aircraft. We sat in the pebbled court near the familiar plashing of the fountain and breathed and drank before redescending into chaos. The footmen were strange anachronisms as they stood about, seemingly unperturbed, yet speaking in hushed tones together in their liveries and silver buttons and we already so dirty from our one night in the noisy woods.

But we left Paris. I have not seen the Lieutenant since and though he was but thirty, this is his third war and I expect he's too experienced a campaigner to be dead.

We left Corbéville and drove all night a few feet apart staring through the darkness at the small white square on the rear step of the preceding ambulance.

The next morning near Avize I staggered from my ambulance to sleep in a field under diagonal sun rays—and I had a dream of a new St. George and the Dragon, of an infantryman dodging from one side to the other of a haystack rising at the center of a vast empty field as an airplane wheeled and dived to sow the ground with its dragon's teeth. He sighted his rifle through the hay with his clear blue eye and fired. I awoke lying on my back, my head throbbing with the heat. I dragged myself to my feet and walked to a wall and found it to be that about a grave yard and reluctantly turned away from the cool water running there. A farm was further down the road, and a woman standing in the garden. Her name was Madame Minost—I have her card.

"Yes, we have water and my husband has made a shower and after you have bathed will you have some wine?"

The shower was a crude affair but worked admirably and with the cold water running on my head I watched the road where peasants were defiling in wagons with cows walking awkwardly at the back, their necks pulled out straight in their halters. I was asked into the dining room and sat with the husband and wife to partake of a vin Mousseux and LuLu biscuits from a tin box. They were very kind and said, "We would rather have you drink our wine than the Germans." Soon I left to rejoin the column which was leaving for Sézanne, and as I said goodbye I realized that understanding is in the least farewell of war.

About the Gothic church of Sézanne, protected with piles of sandbags, the square was filled with soldiers just come from the Line. With bristling beards and smelling of pinard, they pushed about the zinc bars of the cafés to order Pernods and Calvados before turning South on the endless, dotted roads.

Before the station the lines were encumbered with trains and in the sand-bagged arch of the church door I watched the bombers as they wheeled about the town until driven away by anti-aircraft fire, the black bursts appearing among them and remaining undispersed in the windless air.

Soon we drove out a bit and parked in column in a field under branches and ate sardines and two-day-old bread. Nearby in a village café we got some coffee but little else, and we sat with soldiers just from the fighting line, "But how do you expect to have matériel?" I said to an artilleryman in answer to his cry which echoed over France: "How do you expect to have matériel if you worked but forty hours in the week?"

A staff car had arrived, a Polish captain had stepped out and said, "You are to report North at Avize to establish a liaison with the First Tank Brigade. I will leave you my aide, a French sergeant who will direct you." And saluting awkwardly as he stepped backward into the car, he soon jolted off in the little drab Citroën.

I took the Frenchman in my ambulance. He was an Alsatian with a German accent and a shoe manufacturer by profession. Along the night-blown road we drove. "Convoi! Convoi!" I yelled at remnants of retreating batteries of seventy-fives, the steel rims of their wooden wheels knocking up sparks from the road. On either side were Senegalese huddled on the limbers and the caissons.

It was often said the French might stop the tanks with seventy-fives since the 37-and 52-millimeter anti-tank guns were ineffective at piercing the too-heavy armor of the Nazi tanks. The statement was a fallacy disseminated by the French propaganda in seeking to dissimulate the fact that there were not enough anti-tank guns, a much more efficient weapon despite the smaller calibres to pit against a tank than the cumbersome seventy-fives, with their small arc of fire and their obsolete carriages, provided with no supply of armor-piercing shells.

A Panzer division, maintaining its flanks with artillery, had pushed a salient on either hand and the horizon was lurid on three sides and the air echoing with the reverberations of fire.

At Avize, the sergeant jumped down from my ambulance and the column proceeded into the town. Three soldiers, their faces blue in the light of parachute flares, were drinking from the jagged mouths of champagne bottles, the liquid glistening on their cheeks and necks as they raised the bottles to their lips, their eyes luminous from the electric blueness of the air. Avize had been evacuated and we stood on the hill and watched shells dropping in the lower part of the town.

"We are staying till the Germans arrive," the soldiers announced. "Why are you here?" We faced one another in the hot blue light, and our column turned and we proceeded down the narrowing black corridor with its brightening walls of flame.

Later we discovered the Polish Staff Captain and the French Sergeant to be Fifth Columnists and remembered the Captain's salute had not been with two fingers as in the Polish Army. If *they* took such pains over twelve ambulances, one may imagine the efforts taken with brigades.

We drove back some twenty kilometers and spent the remainder of the night in our ambulances sleeping on our unused stretchers. The impression one received was that of sleeping in a *wagon-lits*, the *wagons-lits* of the Sud-Express.

We awoke to find ourselves near deserted farm yards where a few dogs wandered dejectedly, and soon we left them.

Over my motor I heard machine-gun fire, we stopped and dove through a thorn hedge to lie face downward, our mouths in the moss, as a Messerschmitt strafed the road.

We rose and gingerly made our way back through the thorn hedge to join up with another column. I remember jolting behind a small truck mounting an anti-aircraft gun and seeing the bronze teeth of bullets protruding from the breech....

...We aligned ourselves to the South of Sézanne. We watched planes strafe a nearby road, the Messerschmitts falling low along the poplars, and two flights of forty-five bombers, undisturbed by the black puffs of antiaircraft bursts about them, fly over the town to the West and Paris. Panic was in the air, unseeing fear and the madness of flight.

Soon along the road came a car and lying in the arms of an old man was a youth, his face beatic and his belly swathed in bandages.

He had been machine-gunned a mile down the road. We carried him to our ambulances. "And where is a base hospital?" we asked of a passing French ambulance.

"Moved to Troyes, 100 kilometers South." "Are you going?"

"Yes."

"Where are the Germans?"

"God knows! Ask the staff headquarters." The driver of the French ambulance threw the phrase over his shoulder with a sour laugh, for he knew, as we, that the staff had left that morning.

No one was left in Sézanne save the very old and the last train of flat cars was pulling out of the station and still we waited, and as we waited I imagined the boy dying in the pharmaceutic stench of the ambulance with his bowels on the floor beside him.

Wielopolski, our liaison officer, had received an order to establish a contact with the First Tank Brigade at the Château of Verécule, to the North of Sézanne at 2:00 P.M. the same afternoon. It was now noon, Sézanne evacuated, and no Allied troops between us and advancing German tanks.

Yet soon we saw a column of clean infantry advancing with heavy machine guns in mule carts and felt cheered, cheered till at Sézanne they turned East. The liaison officer left in our staff car to go I know not where with one of our drivers. (Recently I was reading *Life*, this five months later, and I saw his picture—his name was Clark—with the inscription that he had been made a prisoner and had but just been released.)

We lunched on dry meat and red wine, drinking from zinc cups with reservists wearing the wound and service stripes with the sky blue of the last war. They were detailed to guard a gasoline depot with pin bayonets on the ends of their ancient rifles, yet they were a better weapon than the wretched, heavy carbine supplied the French, a cheap weapon with its cheap bluing and cheaper stock, and the bayonet one drew from beneath the barrel. Past us walked the rear guard of a beaten mob, and we waited.

Schulze decided it unwise to send the entire column North and he and I left the others with orders that they turn South and we drove North into the hot forests of Verécule.

We passed the station and the train had left, the smoke from the locomotive visible far down the lines, and the streets were littered with rifles, the shop doors hanging open and the church sightless. Up the curving summer-hot road we drove and down the rutted kilometer-long drive to Verécule.

The château stood in the sunlight, abandoned rifles heaped before the half-shuttered windows, the windowpanes bright with the sun, and great black flies buzzed about half-finished meals and heaps of bloody clothing cut from the wounded, for Verécule had been a field hospital. To the rear I went and heard a noise and ventured within to find a deserted *dogue de Bordeaux*, a splendid big brown beast. Of his own accord he followed me back and jumped into the ambulance. I kept him till I lost him at Angers, feeding him on chocolate and sardines and stale bread, our fare for four days.

We chose rifles and unwrapped bullets from the cheap blue papers in which the clips were tied and thought of evacuated Sézanne below us and the Germans somewhere near us, and waited.

Through the underbrush four men came running, their faces haggard and their mouths running with blood. Seeing us, they stopped, then stumbled to where we stood, shouting, "The Germans are behind us machine-gunning from light tanks."

We took them in the ambulances and down to Sézanne, lying abandoned with its sewers flowing over the cobbled streets, the stores gutted and the cobbled streets littered with equipment.

The troops had thrown down their weapons and laden themselves with tinned food which was all that was left in the stores. Later I saw a man in such haste to enter my ambulance that having difficulty in entering because of his pack filled with looted tins he threw it off into the road, and the bicycle he had ridden had not fallen to the ground before it was seized by another.

In the middle of the square of Sézanne, surrounded by empty bottles and tins and rifles, were two figures leaning against the fountain, the water glinting in the sun as it poured from a leaden pipe into the stone bowl.

Of these one was a lieutenant, the other a sergeant. They made no movement save to stare at us as we stopped beside them.

"For seven days I have retreated and my boots are filled with blood. It is to the point of blowing my brains out."

"My lieutenant" said the other, "you are addressing an American."

"An American?" and his eyes dilated and he said he had volunteered from Bridgeport, Connecticut, where he had lived for four years prior to the war.

"Have you places for us?"

"Of course, of course."

Often we heard this tale, of men retreating and empty trucks dashing past them, not stopping to pick them up and everywhere one heard, "It is the sergeants who command us up there, there is no one else; the officers are all gone." At Sézanne this lieutenant was the highest ranking officer I saw, and at Orléans the streets were thick with majors and colonels in their helmets with the braided straps, and at Bordeaux the roads pullulated with golden képi'd generals.

On the road South of Sézanne stood the column of our ambulances, the crosses painted from their roofs. They had been loaded with gasoline, 150 liters to each in 50 liter *bidons* from the depot, and then the reservists grenaded the store they had guarded, and the black smoke with the swirling red flames underneath rose straight into the windless air.

Ten kilometers further on we caught up with the van of the refugees and five Italian planes were circling overhead machine-gunning the crowded road. Hidden in the bushes, I saw the small fragmentation bombs dropping and felt the deafening concussion of their impact and heard the screams as the earth shook and leaves fell from the trees.

I had Schulze on one side and Bob Newman, who writes for the *New Yorker* and had been in Finland, on the other. I remember Schulze saying, "I don't like war," and I agreed, and Newman said "Finland was a picnic compared with this. At least there the planes flew so high you couldn't see the bombs," And the Englishman we had with us wandered about as if he didn't care. We were crouched among little trees on a steep hill by the road and I hoisted myself on a little tree to keep from slipping and shook the foliage. A French reservist cursed me to be still and I looked up and above me was an Italian plane at a hundred yard's altitude, and no one shot at it and all one heard was the horrible dryness, the sharpness and most conclusive sound of planes machine-gunning and it was as if every shot went through the nerves of one's teeth and I knew war to be a simple thing consisting in steel piercing one and leaving round purple holes quite impersonally or rather with the filthy leer of machines and I opened my trousers and pissed down the hill.

Soon, their ammunition expended, they left, unimpaired by Allied aviation or anti-aircraft fire. Blood and bodies littered the roads and feebly kicking horses bleeding from immense wounds and their nostrils. The air was thick with the stench of burning flesh and shrieks. The groans in our ambulances gave way to the musty smell of death.

A medical corps lieutenant was beside me and his eyes were glazed with fear and he drooled from the corner of his mouth as he said, "I haven't slept or eaten for a week." And the soldiers behind taunted him and said:

"You are afraid, my lieutenant?"

And to one another, "My lieutenant is afraid," and then they laughed and swore or groaned. Soon he couldn't stand it and got out.

At Nogent-Sur-Seine the refugees were streaming across a narrow stone bridge. Nearby a group of French officers, standing near an anti-aircraft machine gun, anxiously scanned the sky. Overhead circled a solitary dive bomber. The flat boats were being scuttled up and down the elm-bordered Seine and to the dull explosions I drank a bottle of champagne with Henry Williams, a fellow driver. The girl serving us had tears in her eyes, seeing as she did the wretched, crushed and bloody refugees streaming past. "It is awful, awful," she repeated in dull refrain. Overhead we heard the motor of the circling plane.

Schulze had slung a rifle over his shoulder and we dissuaded him from going back in search of two others—Mock and another who were lost—thus four from our thirteen were lost and five cars one way or another. Young, another driver, an immense man, swam near a flat boat in the Seine and was blown clear of the water as a *péniche* or flat boat was scuttled.

Near a shed where we bandaged refugees, I spoke with a French motorcyclist, a Breton with a face like a rock and Oriental eyes. He showed me his sidecar pierced by two machine-gun bullets and on which he had painted *Le Vengeur—The Revenger* indeed.

"And that crease in your fender?"

"That is where they turned the anti-tank guns on me."

The mortality among these motorcyclists was as great as among the pursuit pilots since often they would run head on into a German column and certainly nothing could be more heart stopping than to meet an armored car at the bend of a highway, to turn, with the one in the side car aiming at the turret slits as the shells passed one, *whiish, whiish.* Such was the adventure of *Le Vengeur*, and when the fender of the side car wheel was creased, the shell not exploding, the *Vengeur* was thrown a foot into the air.

"Au revoir, *Le Vengeur*!"

We dined at a hotel. A mustached Frenchman said that the Germans could come but we would eat, and we did and very well. I filled my pockets with cigarettes and gave them to soldiers clinging to Paris auto-buses used in the work of evacuation from near Paris.

"How did you lose your eye, mon ami?"

"Powder burns."

"Too bad, here, good luck!"

"Merci, merci, mon lieutenant!" and with one arm through the hand rail he lit a cigarette, and the auto-bus, momentarily stopped, rolled on.

On the strangely deserted road to Romilly leading Southeast, we saw a French motorcycle coming toward us at great speed, with an officer seated in the side car. The driver slowed his machine and the officer gestured wildly to stop and shouted, "Romilly has been in the hands of the Germans for two hours!"

Schulze's order to proceed to Romilly was marked as having been issued an hour before, which in itself denoted a complete breakdown of the liaison in that region.

We turned off the main road. South in the twilight to Sens we drove through crowded villages, among scattered troops of Belgians, Poles, and French, weaponless, and, for the most part uncaring since they felt beaten and expressed it in repeating, "Nous sommes trahis! We are betrayed!" Save for one whom I saw with a shotgun over his shoulder surrounded by friends who explained, "He was captured, stole the shotgun, shot three Germans and escaped!" The man grinned, hitched the gun on his shoulder and looked away in the embarrassment of his pleasure.

"Un brave!"

Southwest we drove to Sens on dusty byways, the roads appearing white in the twilight.

It was about the fifteenth or sixteenth of June and I had heard from some reliable source that Paris was fallen, and rolling through a village I was determined to see what effect the news might have. Stopping for a moment before crossing one of the National roads radiating to the South from Paris, I said to a solitary woman, "You know, Paris is fallen." Without a moment of hesitation she said, "Liar." If I'd said as much in a large group I might well have been dragged from my ambulance and shot for a Fifth Columnist.

We spent the night in the square of Sens, eating at a canteen which was jammed with refugees at two in the morning and then filled our ambulance tanks with gas from our Sézanne store by means of a funnel borrowed from a Paris auto-bus stationed nearby between the trees. A lady came up to me, a Mademoiselle de la Chapelle, to entrust to me her cases of Red Cross material. I soon discovered she was the sister-in-law of the Comtesse de la Chapelle whose apartment I had rented in the Avenue Victor Hugo. Another woman pled for transportation South and when Schulze said he would find a place for her, she embraced him and wept with relief—she was not pretty. Her little boy cried when he could not take his new bicycle with him. Another woman implored us to deviate fifteen kilometers from our road to pick up a woman who was in labor. We refused since we considered she would be better off in her bed, and we explained with strained kindness to the hysterical woman that she must pull herself together and that the Germans would not eat her. A convent servant came, her chignon undone, commanding us to take fifty nuns.

On the way through Orléans we saw members of the Volunteer Ambulance Corps looking very trim and suitably regimented and they gave us some red wine and we proceeded Southwest to Tours. By the Loire at two gasoline pumps waited three solid kilometers of cars in file. A journalist of my acquaintance said that three months before he had seen the same thing with the pump owner sitting out in front with a Bleu cigarette dangling from his mouth and his wife swinging the handle of the gas pump, her heavy leather purse hanging over her stomach, and half way down the line, about five hundred meters away, was a splendid car with a tricolor guidon on the fender. The journalist asked of the gas pump owner, "Who is in that car with the tricolor guidon on the fender?" and the man had answered, "That? I believe it is General Gamelin on his way to battle."

While passing through the streets of Tours, a driver was asleep beside me with Sézanne, my *dogue de Bordeaux*, who preserved an equable temper and health despite a diet of bread, sardines and chocolate sprinkled with a little wine, and the driver's head lolling from the window led people to think he was wounded and our column was rushed through. Yet on the outskirts we stopped to watch the dog-fighting going on above Tours and to get out of the way of falling D. C. A. shells, and we flattened ourselves against the houses.

We were able to travel very fast on this road since we had it to ourselves with the exception of a few retreating tanks which would not pull over, not hearing our horns above the din of their caterpillars on the hard road.

And soon we were in Angers. There Schulze put us up at the Embassy where Stanislaus, the factotum resplendent in his buttons bearing the United States seal, gave us to eat and we bathed and shaved and four Polish soldiers whom we had found on the road helped us to wash our shirts. These fellows were what remained of their company, annihilated while serving an anti-tank battery—the Nazi planes strafed and bombed them and they were unable to recover in time to halt the light tanks. "If we but had grenades, all of us might have gotten out, or at least more," they added, lowering their heads.

At the Ministry just opposite, which I had visited some months before, we were informed that our Black Brigade had been annihilated on the flank of the principal German salient North of Avize. From Avize to Sézanne to Nogent-Sur-Seine and finally Romilly, we had been on the fringes of the salient inadvertently for about a week.

I decided that I should go to the Franco-Polish Mission near Dimé the next afternoon to discover if those gentlemen had news of the new ambulances which were overdue.

And the interim I passed with the others in drinking new wine with the concierge of the Embassy who was immensely proud of his son and spoke much of him and rightly since he was a major—the concierge had been a private in the last war and had an unhealed wound from Verdun under his shirt. He said it had begun to improve in September and we dissuaded him from showing it to us. To him I entrusted Sézanne, and there the dog remains, safe in his acquired American citizenship for aught I know. He was a good dog, and I remember promenading with him on a shortened chain purchased at Nogent watching Angers in the throes of evacuation and listening to the tragic notes of the

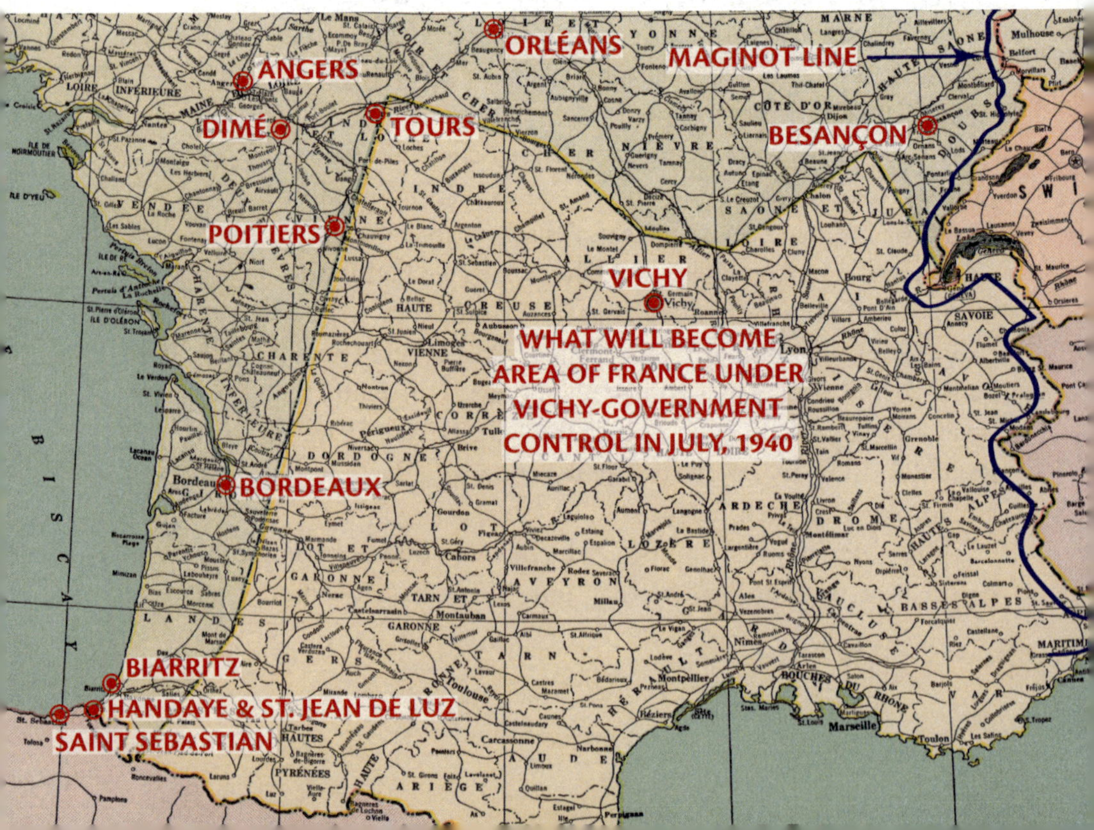

Marseillaise on the radio, and the blaring voice of the Germans saying Angers was to be sky-ignited and razed with the dust under a shower of steel.

The next morning Mock and the other turned up. They had proceeded East, South of Troyes, as far as Besançon, where they said the Nazis had cracked the Maginot Line. They were spotted with dried blood and there was a half-inch of caked gore on the bottom of their ambulances. I went into the sun-hot garden and the streets were silent beyond the walls save for the radio and the tortured *Marseillaise* and I felt my bowels twisting in me and I cursed myself for thinking of the bits of human beings of mincemeat Mock and the other had collected in bags after a bombing.

On our way South to Dimé, according to plan, I turned off from the column to visit the secret quarters of the Franco-Polish Mission. The bridges of the Loire were mined and were scheduled to be blown up the same night at ten. The highroad leading in and out of every little village was half-blocked with attempts at forming anti-tank barrages as in Holland. Sometimes wagons were placed in the highway, and at each of these stood men in civilian clothes armed with ancient rifles and in some cases shotguns. My permit was printed in Polish and filled out in French and so far as these embattled peasants reminiscent of our Minutemen were concerned, I might have been a Fifth Columnist with the rear of the ambulance filled with German soldiers, but I got through safely enough. Occasionally, on the other side, I had seen columns of infantry hastily assembled to be incorporated into the Army of the Loire and I thought of Napoleon. On being approached at Waterloo with the suggestion that he reform on the Loire he mused and answered, "No. When the French are beaten, they are nothing."

On arriving at the little château where the Mission was encamped, I saw tents at either side under the trees and to the white post which had once supported a seesaw which lay beside it in the grass was attached a submachine gun for use against strafing planes. On the sweeping lawn it was mounted in a position untenable in the event of actual attack, which was in keeping with their polished fingernails.

Since they gave me no news, I had rather hoped they would give me something to eat but they didn't and I proceeded back to Dimé.

There I had a most pleasant time in a little farm sharing a mess with the officers and a room with a major and lieutenant under the hospitable eye of a most charitable and unafraid woman. She was a poet and had decorated her little rustic garden with slate plaques in which were cut some of her verses, charming in their naive belief in beauty. The food was excellent and I had my much battered tunic washed and soon felt myself to be a new man. I remember well the ugly yet sympathetic room with its bad Empire beds and the beaded lampshades and orange wall papers, yet the house with its deep terrace bordered with cypresses was in itself old and comfortable and had warmth deep within its walls.

I passed four soldiers standing outside a barn yelling to someone within and soon a sergeant came out looking well satisfied and one of the four entered to take his place. There was much such on the roads and in the billeted villages but with death on every side and the living perpetually in close quarters it could not be helped. I remember speaking to an elderly veteran on the subject—he was an officer of the Legion of Honor and had lost an arm in 1915 and had been on the road from his estate in Picardy for two weeks. "Que voulez vous," he said and shrugged, and I thought of my friend in Tourraine whose gardener was the son of a Uhlan of 1870. It is to be surmised there will be many more such.

Soon we saw all the men at ease in the field being harangued by a colonel and I knew that we were soon to move, since my major and lieutenant room-mates packed up their things and seemed preoccupied. Men were crammed into our ambulances in violation of the international rule that ambulances shall not be used for military purposes. One of our drivers was furious at this and the men grumbled and said that he should not treat them like animals,

I explained to placate them that if they were caught, they would be prisoners while we should be shot—though it was rumored the Germans shot the Poles on sight since the Poles took no prisoners themselves. What I said was true and moreover should we be found armed, which we were, the arm would be pointed at our forehead and the trigger pulled. Should the weapon be loaded it was unfortunate, if not we were prisoners, an instance of the Nazis resorting to applied Biblical justice in their war. Many Polish officers of the medical corps did not wear their white bands with the red crosses on their left arms but rather their pistols. "It is worth more," they would remark with a pat on the holster.

We proceeded to near Poitiers, and determined to get a meal, I went into town and drove to the top of the city to have dinner at the Chapon Fin where I had known the maître d'hôtel. I succeeded in making my way in though the place was jammed. One ended by paying more and more attention to one's stomach. I slept through the bombing of the station.

The next day, having rejoined the others and since we had no function, I decided to go down to Bordeaux one day ahead of the others to see about the ambulances which might well be arriving in this chaos with their neophyte drivers and no one to receive them or explain where they must go or what they must do. I went to the station with my military railroad pass given me by the Franco-Polish Mission, but it was of no avail, the trains being immobilized. I went to the local colonel with the hope of requisitioning a motorcycle or permission to accompany some officer going down.

"No, no one is to go to Bordeaux."

"But what am I to do, mon colonel?"

"Obey your orders."

I saluted and left, pondering what to do when I saw as a *deus ex machina*, Stanislaus of the Embassy at Angers in a battered car yet bearing yellow diplomatic license plates. I flagged him and rode backward on a heap of luggage into Bordeaux on the eve of the bombing.

From the American Consulate, I telephoned Mrs. Biddle to tell her Ted would be in the next day and to express my admiration for the leadership and cool judgment he had at all times expressed under fire. We all admired him. Of the Poles embarking for England near St. Jean de Luze, three of the drivers elected to follow Schulze who became a lieutenant of Polish Cavalry in Scotland, some to remain in France. Of these an artist, whose name escapes me, and who looked like a Renaissance Borgia with his short tawny beard and fawn ears, said it was only in France he could live. The rest, I included, returned to America.

IBERIAN FINALE

NOW THAT I have come to the logical conclusion of this book I must narrate the slow regression to normalcy and mediocrity, the letting down to trivial emotions, and the unmeaningness of casual life. All this not before the bombing, but slowly as old fears reasserted themselves. My uniform, which I was to wear with one exception for three more weeks for lack of anything better, slowly lost its significance, and the diapason of sensation was lost in a dull cycle of routine. I will state humbly yet truthfully what I know to be heresy that in war maybe found an end other than death.

At the Consulate they had heard nothing of the arrival of a ship from America, and it was only later that I was to learn the ambulances were that day on the high seas on an English ship. When France fell, she turned her bows to England where the section she carried is being operated. Later, from Lisbon, I sent a cablegram to Schulze asking if he would command it in the field since all his ambulances with numberless Rolls Royces, Hispanos, Bentleys, Bugattis, Lagos, Cadillacs and lesser cars were left on the docks of Bordeaux.

It was impossible to find a room, yet inured to sleeping anywhere I was undismayed. At the Splendide I ran into Mrs. Briggs and soon Maloney and Pamp, and later Miss Henrietta Ely, then

Paul Ghali, Mr. Edgar Mowrer, Monsieur de la Tournelle, who had but just become engaged to Colette de la Ville Rabelle (such decorum seemed to me superfluous). Virtually everyone I have mentioned in these pages was there though I did not see them all—it was like the finale of a musical comedy.

I soon found a cot through the kindness of Mrs. Briggs in a room set apart for the use of Americans by the American Red Cross.

I was given the address, and at eleven walked in off the street into a dark room filled with cots on most of which were figures sleeping. No sooner was I in bed that I heard a violent cannonading and the alarms started their crescendo. People awoke and someone yelled, "Du calm," and people shifted about. I put my clothes back on and went to look out, but came back in the house when I saw bursts directly overhead. Soon from the *raum raum* of the motors I heard descending a *wheeeeesh-boom* and the floor shook and the glass rattled in the doors. I muttered, "Screecher bombs," and got back into bed. They are ghastly things since one can hear them descending from the skies but one knows not where they fall and every bomb is for one's self. Bordeaux had no subterranean shelters, since the water was but a few feet below the surface of the streets, and the public shelters in the big squares were but trenches superimposed on the ground with sand-bag walls completely open at the top. They were protection against nothing but flying splinters. By chance a bomb landed directly on one of these open shelters and it was a mess.

I lay listening and Mr. Mowrer a few blocks away stated in his dispatch the next morning that he had counted some one hundred and twenty heavy bombs—quite a number for June, 1940.

Soon the floor heaved and there was a tremendous concussion and much shouting as a house came down a block away. Then we were left alone. It had lasted an hour and the planes were supposedly Italian and had flown above just to show the French Government the Axis wasn't fooling. I am sure an entire government—Executive, Legislative, Army, Navy—as well as the countless Embassies and private citizens of note have never before been simultaneously subjected to such an attack. Certainly there was later not much resistance to the peace and this "psychological" bombing may have had much to do with unanimity in armistice.

The next morning I passed the house which had been hit, of three stories, it was nothing but a pile of rubble in which a few soldiers were seeking for bodies, and there I saw my friend of the Ministry of the Interior, he of the *tarte maison and l'affaire* Baronne Z.

"How many?" I said, shaking his hand and indicating the pile with my head.

"Eleven," he answered.

It was only later I remembered neither of us had indicated any surprise at seeing the other.

There was a pastry shop just opposite, and I went in to buy a *croissant* and a cup of chocolate.

"Did you know them?"

"Ah yes, they were *concurrents*, business rivals."

"What will you do when the Germans arrive tomorrow?"

"Que faire? Receive them with a smile." I slammed the door behind me.

At an *épicerie* I purchased a lot of tinned goods and, on coming out, I saw Schulze, just arriving. I gave him his mother's address, he grinned and said, "Quite a night you had." I said yes and smiled. It was the last I saw of him.

Mr. Mowrer, whom I met at the Splendide, advised me to get a suit of civilian clothes and asked me to write an article to give to him duly passed by the censor by lunchtime. The Bureau of Censorship was in the famous colonnaded opera house which Garnier took as his model for that in Paris. After writing the following article, I had it censored among the gilt and columns. No words were deleted. I assume they were merely illegible and wonder when I read in the press today that a paragraph was censored whether or no it actually was, or someone just lazy:

"Bordeaux, June 21—For a week I was at the apex of the wedge of the German advance Southeast of Paris, always just out of reach of the swiftly moving Panzer divisions (armored divisions)...

"...Black flies buzzed about bloody heaps of clothing and half-finished meals on the tables under the trees of the deserted château. The silence was oppressive as we waited in the noon heat, two kilometers beyond Sézanne, to establish a liaison with the First Tank Brigade of the Polish Army.

"In the valley below us the town had been evacuated and the stores were looted and the streets littered with abandoned rifles and knapsacks.

"The Polish liaison officer, now disappeared, had urged that the entire column go up to the château to establish contact, but the lieutenant (one word censored) had thought it unwise to send all the ambulances toward the Nazis and he and I stood alone waiting in the silence.

"Suddenly we heard men breaking through the forests and three French soldiers without rifles, helmets or equipment, their faces haggard and full of blood, burst through the underbrush shrieking to us that German tanks were machine-gunning the roads 500 meters behind them. We took them in our ambulance and rolled through Sézanne to rejoin our column, which was aligned on the straight road to Nogent-Sur-Seine. The air was hot with burning gas depots which reservists in their sky-blue uniforms had grenaded.

"We caught the van of the refugees. Soon five Italian planes whose colors were visible at their low altitude were circling overhead machine-gunning the crowded road. Hidden in the bushes, I saw the bombs dropping and felt the deafening concussion of their impact and heard the screams. The earth shook and leaves fell from the trees.

"Soon, their ammunition expended, they left, unimpaired by Allied aviation or anti-aircraft fire. Bleeding bodies of men, women and children littered the roads beside their feebly kicking horses. A burning woman lay by a truck. I tugged at her arm and it came off in my hand. The air was thick with the stench of burning flesh and shrieks. (Two lines censored)."

On seeing the above in the *Chicago Daily News* my friend, Jozef Staniewicz, of the Polish Consulate in Chicago, sent the article post haste to Mother. It was the first news she had of me since I left Paris.

I said to the censor (whom I noted was dressed oddly enough in an aviation corporal's uniform) when I saw him read the part about the arm, "I hope that will shake them up at home." "Too late," he answered without raising his eyes. I saw him in Lisbon a week later in a natty sports outfit.

And then I went to purchase my suit—one of pure sartorial horror, since I did not want to spend more than was absolutely necessary of the dollars I kept in my money belt. The trousers were gigantic at the bottom. I remember putting them on in the lavatory while waiting at the Ministry of the Press for an exit visa. A fellow came in, a poor distracted creature who discovered himself to be the German Traitor-in-France for the radio. Of course he could not get a Spanish visa and he asked me as an impartial American what to do. I advised him to go to England if they would have him. Certainly in Bordeaux his miserable life wasn't worth two sous.

An hour later, while waiting for Mr. Mowrer and food at the Splendide, I noted:

"I have been thrown from the regorging roads of France into the static ebullience of Bordeaux. I sit on the terrace of the Hôtel Splendide considering myself most fortunate at having a table and with all of France I wait for food, for at least one finds one's self in eating. Though I feel the presence of the end, I hardly care.

"An hour before I saw Reynaud running hatless through the streets and as I think dully of this, not dully perhaps but rather in the mood of one who has come early for a show, has come through the tooting impersonality of traffic in the storm and now arranges himself in his seat and perhaps listens with one ear to conversation about him, I wait at the Splendide and listen to the clatter and gurgle of all these once important people about me, and to my right a voice rumored 'They' had extinguished the flame of the Unknown Soldier—expressions of odium in triviality. I shift in my chair.

"But I am hungry. The service is quite understandably abominable, yet to such an extent that I trouble to complain to the maître d'hôtel. With all of France I wait an hour for my food and from functional habit become irascible. Yet the maître d'hôtel is a fine fellow with the yellow and green ribbon of the Médaille Militaire in his buttonhole; when I told him I had waited an hour and one half and had been served nothing, he looked at my dirty uniform and seized the pimpled, adolescent waiter, shook him till he dropped what he held, and as he stooped the maître d'hôtel booted him and shouted, his eyes flashing, his finger in the air, "Wait, the Boches will teach you to serve when they come tomorrow!" Old France and new.

...I feel a surge of fellowship for this man, a vestige of the France I loved; a Frenchman whose ability to cooperate was not perverted by misconceptions of individualism; the Grognard of Napoleon's legions, the Poilu of the last war, a man whose patriotism isn't rotted with political agnosticism, in short, a man fit to live in France. The patriotism he feels so inherently must be a mysticism of faith in the man intellectually qualified to be a leader. France has none such, alas.

"My numbed hope is evanescent. A vision of the France I love passes in my mind rife with Napoleonic legend, the screaming of Meissoniac eagles, and a tricolor it was worth dying for, I feel it is more important for a nation to conserve its reason to die than to have reason to live."

And then I wrote on the paper napkin before me with the red pencil drawn from my map-case a final lyrically unfortunate regurgitation of emotion, a pot pourri of what I had heard and felt—a vomiting of emotional nausea:

A Nazi foot stamped out the Flame;
The Light is now extinct, your giant Arch unwarm'd
In Glory's breath weighs on Metropolis,
Oui, Triumph's legend bearing pediments
Survey Lutetia pandered by her sons.
Brown leaves from Laurel wreaths are in the wind.
I weep.
Elba, St. Helena, Paris;
Exiled thrice,
Beneath your spired dome
Voluted porphyry is goal.
Why are your Eagles not unchained to scream
Their tricolors to crepitate, their fringe
To flame on hot winds from sky-ignited *Capitale*?
An Apotheosis of Lutitian pyres!
Cathedrals crash in martyric fires!
Gutters run in palace zinc....
Unrazed monuments are monuments of shame,
Unburnt altars, sacrilege.

And then with all of France I put these thoughts away for the meal had come at last.

Mr. Mowrer arrived with Ghali, and they were deep in plans of how they should leave France. Mr. Mowrer at one time considered swimming out to the British warships off St-Jean-de-Luze, at another of crossing the Pyrénées into Spain by mountain paths; these alternatives to be adopted at the last moment and as a last expedient. I considered the first but did not envy him the second for one might be shot down by a mountain sentry and in any event the roads were difficult. I remembered crossing the mountains four years before on a path so winding that a Ford must be backed around the corners. Owls had flown to break their necks against the windshield, for it was at night, and later a storm which put the deluge to shame.

In any event, I needed visas and a Spanish one was not granted without a Portuguese one since none but a transit visa might be given, and the Portuguese not without an American passport or visa for some country other than Portugal. In other words the hospitality of Spain and Portugal was given but grudgingly since neither were said to have much food, and one must of course first procure a *visa de sortie*, or exit visa, from France. This I had done through Monsieur de la Tournelle of the Press Bureau who was happy in the thought of impending matrimony. I was amazed that one could think of such things. All which the bureaus now possessed were their personnel and rubber stamps and a few sheets of official note paper. They were indescribably difficult to find since the man in the street had not the vaguest notion where the departments of government might be, yet all was discovered by hearsay.

As I looked up to see a French pursuit plane, a Devoitine, stunting over Bordeaux at a low altitude so that the exhaust was visible as it issued from the ports, I ran directly into Miss Henrietta Ely, resplendent in her uniform. We discovered we were both on our way to the Portuguese Consulate.

We were met with chaos badly administered by two French *deuxième classe* privates. All afternoon we sat in line despite papers with official seals the American Consul had given us presenting his compliments to the Portuguese Consul and asking that we be admitted.

The next morning we waited again, philosophically and without humor, till disgusted we ceased and Miss Ely went to find a captain friend of hers to whom she had given the trailer she had used with such success near her Vertès decorated officers' mess at Metz. With papers from the Central Bureau of Circulation he passed through the guards and by a Senator who was weakly saying, "Mais je suis Sénateur," and showing his *tarte maison* unavailingly to the guards. It was not a pretty thing this mess with everyone shouldering and acting like pigs and seeking to evoke dead authority at the gates of the Portuguese Consulate. Inside we were informed the consul was at lunch, but at least we were inside in the cool outer chamber, and we felt much was accomplished. Soon we had our visas and it was fortunate we got them when we did for many of those received later were invalidated at the Portuguese border since the consul had given them beyond his authority and for bribes. Then the captain presented us to a corporal who was a great friend of the Spanish Ambassador and he drove us in his Lincoln Zephyr to the Spanish Consulate where the Ambassador was residing. As we waited outside, the corporal entered to see the Ambassador and soon returned with our passports stamped with two courtesy visas. He told us we were lucky in that the Ambassador was leaving and he pointed at a black Cadillac standing near the entrance with trunks strapped high on the roof and a yellow license plate at the back. Miss Ely gave him a thousand francs "for the poor of his company."

In the central square an aviation lieutenant approached me and told me to put the forage cap I carried tucked in my belt back on my head. I told him I had been demobilized and asked him if he had not more important duties to perform and thought of my cousin Tony de Mores being taught to fold his blanket and brush his teeth in his officers' training camp.

Everywhere I felt a recurrence of that which I had felt in every town which I had seen evacuated, in Avize and Sézanne and Nogent, and Sens; at Tours and Angers and Poitiers and Dimé, the muffled roar of the approaching wave which gave us no surcease.

Miss Ely had a Buick painted in olive drab with a white circle at the back and a square of British gas paint on the hood; a light green paint which turns pink in poison gas so warning the driver of asphyxiants. She had used this Buick at the "Front," and she asked if I wished to travel to Portugal with her for which I was and am most grateful.

We left at eight to sup on the way on a cold egg placed between great halves of bread and wine—a delirium meal. The bread and wine would have been sufficient—the cold egg was grotesque and since it had been fried resembled a malevolent cold eye. Near Biarritz we stopped at dead of night to search for the villa of Miss Ely's psychopathic cook, a villa she had made herself from odds and ends cast up on the beach named the Villa Jeanne; through an endless labyrinth of villas each with a name we went searching for the Villa Jeanne in the darkness which seemed a darkness of the mind. But I was glad enough to find the villa at four in the morning, for we were given beds and the Pekingese Miss Ely had sought to take from France with her was safe—a wretched little beast I would have throttled a hundred times had I not been fond of its mistress. Miss Ely was extraordinary and, possessing authentic British phlegm, she could brazen out anyone by putting on a remarkably natural show of being stupid looking the while so respectable that the officials waved her by with a tired sigh and I likewise. She would have made an excellent spy but perhaps she had too much of a sense of humor for that, for she was funny in many ways. I shall always remember with sympathy her avowal that she had left the family silver in order to leave place for two magnums of champagne, but the possibility of being overtaken by Panzer divisions after we had taken so much trouble to legalize our flight all for a little dog that snorted like a baby—no, I was not sympathetic.

So thus we arrived at Handaye in the daubed Buick, Miss Ely in her regimentals and I in my unesthetic suit with the large trouser bottoms, the rear of the Buick bulging with Evian bottles and champagne, tins of food I had purchased, and Miss Ely's many bags and my musette. I felt like a *basso buffo*.

At the bridge we waited twelve hours and I remembered complaining at Le Havre when the *douane* took more than thirty minutes not a year before; I shrugged and took some sardines from the rear and we ate them with our fingers.

We saw a lady watching us from a trim black roadster heaped high in back with Vuitton bags, she looking neat and practical.

Later she said she admired our *sans gêne* and the effective way we ate the sardines with our fingers. She was Mrs. Porter of Chicago, a wondrously clever woman to whom I had a letter of introduction but in Paris failed to use it for some reason I shall never divine and I have often been short with myself at the thought for she was very interesting.

I saw many I knew at the bridge, particularly General Haller looking pale and very old, and for whom I felt a great sympathy.

The atmosphere of Spain was unpleasant, and we were overcome with no sense of relief when once we had penetrated the formalities of having our names compared favorably with those on the black list, the searchings for money while we stood beneath a large photograph of Franco, the cross questionings by lean youths wearing red tassels on their forage caps, and the fire of the Civil War still in their eye. The Gestapo took control of the French frontier twelve hours after we had crossed.

Our first goal was San Sebastian. The great pearls of the lamps surmounting the balustrade glowed uninhibited in the balmy night and the cafés blazed on the Réal. Yet it was a far different city than that which I had visited with my friend Freddy Willems, who was killed in the war, and Washie Irving five years before. I remember when I presented the last named to our literary ambassador at Madrid, Mr. Bowers, and his look of utter astonishment and his words to the effect that the desk which separated us had belonged to Washington Irving and that at the moment it was covered with leaves from his manuscript of a biography of our first and greatest Ambassador to Spain. Certainly Washie's name and mine were an antithesis of popularity in Spain. But Freddy's laugh was everywhere as I sat in the café drinking port and asking of the head waiter which was the best restaurant.

He told me the name of the once fashionable hotel, the name of which I have forgotten. (Was it Hotel Queen Maria Christina?)

Outside on the broad sweep of the drive was parked Lady Mendl's familiar Rolls Royce with the wickered body and a great trunk at the back. "No, Peter, this is not for you," I said to myself and turned to enjoy black bread—there is no white bread in Spain—and *ternero* or ubiquitous calf at a restaurant. I noticed everywhere hung Nazi flags and opposite the British Consulate intermingled with the exhortations of the Falangist posters stating "Gibraltar por la España," and one could imagine them being printed in the Wilhelmstrasse.

We had but three days to make our trip, three days in Spain, which we considered adequate and soon we were high in the Sierra near Villa Formosa. All in all it was the most unpleasant part of the year. I would rather experience bombs a hundred times then the uncertain tedium of the forty-eight hours we spent in the no-man's-land high in the mountains between the Spanish and Portuguese frontiers on a plateau as flat as one's hand for several kilometers at either side and always fearful of leaving the car lest the line move up a few feet and we lose our place. This put all my heel kickings on the hard seats of ministries to shame. Waiting is terrible for one cannot hide from one's self the truth that all one's life one waits.

Occasionally some such group as the party of the Duchess of Luxembourg would drive past us raising the dust and our curses, but individuals with diplomatic passports fared no better than we. We should have had nothing to eat—for the most part our tinned supplies were gone—had it not been for the magnificent English who came up to give us food—tea and meat sandwiches and lovely lavender scented but efficient English ladies made special food for the babies and the cricket spirit was in the air and the American Consulate sent us telegrams of cheer. Soon a privy was constructed by the road and I thought it rather like the mountain coming to Mahomet for one had been obliged to walk for miles before finding the least bush one might crouch behind.

I spent the night under the throbbing disc of the Iberian moon and the dew drenched my face in the cold and I was recompensed with a dream of such fragrance as I have never had before or since.

At last we were at Villa Formosa, the Portuguese frontier, where we were hectored by the Chief of the International Police—the grandiloquent name for the Portuguese constabulary—and we received a telegram from Minister Pell saying he would find places for us in Lisbon. This was essential in order to secure permission to enter that town for no one was allowed within its limits who could not prove he had sufficient lodging, for the town was swollen with refugees. To insure our obedience, our passports were taken from us in gross violation of international procedure.

We spent another night in this town, a night of surrealism in which Dali might have rejoiced, for the room which I and one of my companions were forced to share at the local inn, I sleeping on the floor on a mattress which on my examining it for bugs I found to be splotched with blood, was equipped with a tin bidet from which rose like a century plant an opened umbrella and a great vine grew through the window and across the ceiling. All night people passed through our room in mumbling haste banging my head with the door. But the supper had been good. "So the *Bellérophone* might have appeared to Napoleon on his voyage to St. Hélèna," I thought as I endeavored to compose myself despite the pekingese snuffling in my ear.

The next morning I had a shave—the Portuguese seemed a race of barbers and even the poorest does not shave himself—and then went to observe a train. It had been there for two days at the customs and one woman began to scream spasmodically and with the diaphramic rhythm of hysteria and, still imbued with the realism war imposes, I took matters in my own hands and gave her a mighty slap across the face. She stopped.

It was strange how the old fears returned for I drove within the speed limits and was again properly cowed by officials and slept on my back and not on my side as I had during the war, for I have an unexplained fear of sleeping on my side, a fear which grasps me only in somnolence, and once again I found my speech impaired where it had flowed clearly. Stuttering is a strange thing, like a limp—with effort one need not limp, so with perpetual effort until the effort becomes habit one need not stutter, and did I today see an hysterical woman, I believe I would let another, the doctor in the crowd, a policeman or other official slap her. War is paradoxical for there is no doubt it instills self-reliance in clearing the stage for totalitarian government, for war shows how transient are wealth and position and proud names and I think of Bordeaux with the Senateur before the Portuguese Consulate, and the Rolls Royces abandoned, and the fleeing duchesses and the hodgepodge of nationalities and tongues on the plateau of Villa Formosa and all the broken homes and faith left behind and the calm British Consulate to help us and the telegrams bidding us good cheer from the U.S.A. God damn our pacifism!

For some reason, Mr. Pell's message was not recognized and we were allocated to Chaldas-la-Rhaina, a little seaside town where the English and Americans and some French refugees were to be "interned" before their ships sailed—this to distribute the influx of population equably throughout the country.

On the way down through lovely Portugal, we stopped off at Casa las Senhorim where an Englishman had an inn with cottages near it that one might engage for the pigeon shooting, or for golf or tennis. There I met Captain Barrington-White, sometime of the Grenadier Guards and his charming wife who was a Kingsland and cousin to the Harold Kingsland of our Ambulance Committee. I shall be ever grateful to the Captain for his lending me some shirts and socks and I saw much of him later at Estoril while sunning myself on the beach, lunching at noon under a parasol, and reading D. H. Lawrence through dark glasses.

In our cottage we were a disparate group and must have caused much speculation, but we did not care and had long discussions on theosophy in which Mrs. Porter was interested, and I discoursed on my theory on the significance of the mutations of the straight and curved lines, a theory I had set forth with great elaboration and without truculence in my novel.

But soon our limit was up and we must report to the International Police at Chaldas-la-Rhaina and our "concentration camp."

There the routine was always the same for ten days. In the morning, I was awakened in my wretched hotel by the ugly kitchen maids staring in my window as I lay on my straw mattress and I would shriek, "Away with you, you sluts!" And they would giggle and run away—already I was making invidious comparisons—when I had had no mattress, I was happy enough—and soon I had breakfast followed by some excellent port. I was determined to sample all the ports in Portugal so as to not waste my time in *farniente* but now to my surprise I found I could get drunk as I could not in the Army, and then to the International Police to ask if they had heard whether we might proceed to Lisbon, and always the answer was the same. No. It was very heartless this detention without cause or reason and without limit, and did we leave we should be imprisoned. Many women became thin and hysterical.

Soon none but the Americans were left and I discovered through Commander Leigh of the British Consulate that the American Consul, on being asked by the chief of the International Police whether he wanted Americans released, had answered no, that we should be kept away so that his offices would not be overcrowded.

But had it not been for the waiting and the impatience to get into Lisbon to arrange for our tickets and the unutterable boredom, I should have enjoyed Chaldas—certainly the swimming on the vast deserted beaches was excellent and the food plentiful and in unending courses—at our hotel we were always served a fish, fowl, and meat—and at twilight it was pleasant to walk among the cork and palm trees and hear the melancholy notes of the scissor grinders blowing in their pan pipes and to see the women with earthen water jugs on their heads and pass the sloe-eyed girls at their unwatchful waiting in the municipal gardens.

At last everyone had gone save one pathetic English-woman who had lost her husband—he was valet to Calinescu—and we dared not tell her what we thought—and Miss Ely and Mrs. Porter decided to go off despite the possibility of being jailed. Mr. Pell later told me that by so placing themselves without the law he could have done nothing to extricate them had they been jailed—and I received the day's permission to visit Lisbon.

The British Padre, an extraordinarily hospitable man, signed a paper to the effect that he would put me up and with it I went to see the Chief of the International Police. He informed me that he would have me released did I secure confirmation of my good faith from the American Consulate. Confidently I went to see them and found their telephone broken. When I remonstrated the Vice Consul, then recently flown from America, said he could do nothing, that he was working twenty-four hours a day. Two days later I saw his dissipated face in the Casino at Estoril. I went to Minister Pell and was given tea and he very kindly called the Chief of Police and I was released. A tempest in a teapot. Had our consulate a private drawing fund as the British, we would have had no trouble for every man not only had his price in Portugal but it was announced.

While waiting till the *Manhattan* should leave, I stayed at the kind Padre's and wandered in his lovely cemetery, certainly one of the most lovely in Europe where lies that most English of writers, Fielding, and there I met John Frazer and a lady whose name I forget. She was charming and had been attached to the *19ième* Train, a regiment of women ambulance drivers attached to the French Army. She said she was at a château debating with wounded soldiers how many she should take—eight sitting or four lying—when the watcher in the tower shouted that he saw an enemy column. They hid, those who could not walk behind the hedges and

S.S. Manhattan

she in the château with a view of the court. Soon the motorcycles came into the court and the officer said, his voice echoing in the silence of deserted walls, "We know there are French here. Stand up and you shall be prisoners, otherwise you die!" Four wounded French stood up haltingly, bullets issued from the submachine gun and the column with explosions of exhaust wheeled back into the country side.

John Frazer and I went to the cafés and saw the dapper-looking officers in their uniforms very much like the Dutch, and to see the Exhibition, an excellently done thing by the side of the sea—a neutral victim of the war since it was almost empty—and he told me over a dinner in the best restaurant, the Negresco, filled with gobs from Admiral Le Breton's squadron, lying at anchor in the Tagus, that his family had owned cork estates in Portugal for over a hundred years. Though he was but nineteen he directed them himself and told me many interesting things: that the Lisbon street cars, virtually funiculars, were considered the finest in the world, each car being equipped with five brake systems since should a car get loose there was no telling the damage that might be done in the narrow winding streets; that the telephone system in Lisbon as well as most public utilities were British owned; that Portugal had but one anti-aircraft gun and that opposite the President's house, and much about Salazar; but the most interesting thing he said was that at the beginning of the war the British had but one Spitfire—that Sir Samuel Hoare was in Spain to pay the Spanish debt to Italy in order that Spain might not have cause to permit Italian occupation of Ceuta opposite Gibraltar. He asked me to stay over and shoot pigeon with him among his dark cork forests in the mountains. Sometimes I wish I had.

And then the sealed train arrived from Bordeaux and all those we had left behind were there, delightful Morty Singer with long whiskers, but cheerful, and Mrs. Briggs and many others, and the last night before sailing I managed to get a room at the Aviz, the same I had occupied on landing from the Clipper not quite eight months before and I thought of Longues and Paris and Mano and Pierre and Fido and Hubert and Jean and of my cousin in her chateau behind the broken line and all the good ones blown before the awful wind even then ruffling the Atlantic.

The trip back was very pleasant and I shared my cabin with a Major Coburn who had been Military Attaché in Warsaw. The port authorities had the bad taste to let a pursuit plane fly near the ship, and soon I was in New York and by chance ran into Frank and Louisa Griswold opposite the Plaza.

EPILOGUE

PETER DEWEY'S service in the Polish Military Ambulance Corps won him the Croix de Guerre with Bronze Star, the Croix des Combattants, and the highest Polish decoration—the Order of Polonia Restituta. After his return to the United States, he studied law at the University of Virginia, wrote the book to which these notes are an epilogue, and, in 1941, joined the Office of the Coordinator of Inter-American Affairs. In August of that year, he drew up for Nelson Rockefeller a report analyzing the Free French and Vichy French positions in Latin America with respect to propaganda and general cultural influence. In a later memorandum, he recommended that the C.I.A.A. deal directly with the Free French Government in South America. In December, as chief of the minority group section of the Coordinator's Office, he was sent to London to deal with the correlation of French, Polish, and Yugoslav cultural goingson in Latin America. He flew from Baltimore the day before Pearl Harbor. In London he talked with leading Free French, Polish, and Yugoslav officials, and interviewed General de Gaulle. "I urged," Dewey subsequently wrote in a report of his mission, "...that the General, by not permitting the Free French of Latin America to co-operate with the C.I.A.A. (as the result of a non-recognition which must be from the very nature of things temporary) was deserting his countrymen in Latin America to the Germans by refusing them what support we might consider it of mutual benefit to give them, and was placing them in a position where they could do little but accede to Nazi demands." As a result of this interview, General de Gaulle signed and gave to Dewey letters to Free French deputy director generals in the United States urging them to cooperate with the Coordinator's Office.

In August, 1942, Peter entered the Army as a second lieutenant in the Air Transport Command. Subsequently promoted to first lieutenant, he served as an intelligence and liaison officer in French Equatorial Africa, French North Africa, British West Africa, Anglo-Egyptian Sudan, French Somaliland and Arabia. During the course of a luncheon given by General Giraud in Algiers, he was asked by Giraud to be his interpreter on a projected visit to the United States. This bore fruit in July, 1943, when Dewey was sent to Washington on temporary assignment to the Giraud Mission.

A year later, Captain Dewey, then attached to the Office of Strategic Services in Algiers, was made commanding officer, with the acting rank of major, of the Mission Etoile—a behind-the-lines combat-intelligence mission in Southern France. On August 10, 1944, accompanied by a French officer and a French *Battaillon de Choc*, radio operator, he was parachuted from a flying fortress in the first recorded blind drop into this area. The trio was soon joined by two other airborne Etoile groups—eleven men in all. Mission Etoile was notably successful. Over a period of six weeks, working undercover and under the leadership of Major Dewey, it collected and disseminated to Allied H.Q., through the Agency of O.S.S.' Algiers radio station, intelligence concerning enemy order of battle and troop movements, ammunition dumps, air fields, railroad transport, and the F.F.I. political situation. Its reconnaissance contributed materially to the strafing and destruction by the Allied Air Forces and by the F.F.I. of elements of the First and Eighth German Armies. It recruited intelligence agents from the F.F.I. and helped supply the Maquis with equipment from O.S.S. supply drops. It captured 384 prisoners and exfiltrated two American pilots who had been shot down. Peter Dewey's part in all this, which ranged from extricating himself from the pine tree into which he was parachuted, 35 kilometers off the pinpoint intended, to infiltrating retreating German columns in a captured German staff car, thus risking Allied strafing as well as discovery by the enemy, was recognized by the fact that Colonel de Metz, commanding officer of the Deuxième Dragons, a French tank destroyer regiment, invited Mission Etoile to assist at the surrender of 5000 German troops "in recognition of the quality of the intelligence which the mission had supplied"; and by the award of the Legion of Merit to Major Dewey "for exceptionally meritorious conduct in the performance of outstanding services." This medal was presented to him by General Donovan in the spring of 1945. Peter also received from the French Government, for his leadership of Mission Etoile, the Legion of Honor and a second Croix de Guerre, this time with Palm and Star.

At this time, Peter was working on the O.S.S. history project in Washington under the direction of Dr. Conyers Read. He had hoped to return to France, instead, at the time of the Japanese collapse, was sent by O.S.S., as Senior American Authority attached to the Allied Mission in Southern Indo-China, to observe and report on conditions there, particularly for the benefit of the State Department, which had requested O.S.S. to develop intelligence in French Indo-China. "The information contained in his reports," the Director of the Strategic Services Unit of the War Department has written, "was of great value both to O.S.S, and to the State Department."

Peter's death in Saigon occurred nine weeks after he left Washington. "On the afternoon of 26 September 1945," the official report reads, "Colonel Dewey's jeep was stopped by a road-block about 100 yards from O.S.S. headquarters in Saigon. Dewey got out, presumably to identify himself as an American officer, but was killed by Annamese machine-gun fire at point-blank range." In forwarding this report to Peter's father, President Truman wrote: "Please accept my deepest sympathy for the sad death of your gallant son."

Peter had gone to Saigon via Karachi, Calcutta, Kandy, Madras, Rangoon and Bangkok. "We flew in on the first plane to land," he wrote his wife in his last letter. "Our job was to evacuate the prisoners of war—I am commanding officer with the acting rank of Lieutenant-Colonel.... Now that the prisoners have been safely sent out, I remain to represent American interests.... The political situation is immensely complex but one which our group considers but impersonally and objectively since it does not concern us.... The country is incredibly lovely and I have bought thee a green Buddha carved from a tusk—it sounds awful, but it is quite the loveliest one I have ever seen—thin and svelte and covered with waxen flowers and filled with serenity.... These last two weeks have been incredibly exhausting, but I hope soon, oh, my dearest one, that I shall have much more leisure and that soon I shall be home again...."

Peter himself was filled with serenity, and those who saw him in Washington during the last few months before his final mission were sometimes struck by the way in which his conversation touched habitually on his peacetime writing ambitions rather than on his war exploits. His personality included the attributes of a fearless and resourceful man of action and political realist, mature beyond his years, with those of a romantic and an artist. He was unusually perceptive of human motives as well as of esthetics, and it is typical that his Mission Etoile report should have contained, along with a precise chronicle of objectives achieved, equally precise impressions of the French political scene. His insight into things French was matched only by his affection therefore. Peter had an observant humor, style, direction, a talent for friendship, and a real toughness beneath a kind of *ancien-régime* gentility. He was the possessor of a pervasive and unaffected modesty, and, had he been here to edit these brief notes, they would undoubtedly have been briefer.

—GEOFFREY T. HELLMAN

Buddha carving from elephant tusk Peter bought for Nancy

ACKNOWLEDGMENTS

WITH SPECIAL THANKS to Paula Dietz, Beth Gutcheon, Alison Hoppin, and David Schoenbrod for their felicitous editing suggestions; To EB Smith and Jerome d'Anglejan for sharing photographs; to Teofil Lachowicz, Ph.D for identifying both people and actions in my father's photographs of Polish troops.

Ronald Gehrmann, computer guru extraordinaire, who in addition to his constant help, introduced me to the so-talented Sarah Bauhan and Henry James of Bauhan Publishing. It is they who gave this book new life.

In addition, I am very grateful for Philip Taubman's elegant and precise summary of this book and of my father's OSS service—generously given by him for this book's back cover.